Neuromarketing Attributes in the Context of Determinants of
Business Behavior and Neurolinguistic Programming

Róbert Štefko / Zuzana Birknerová, et al.

Neuromarketing Attributes in the Context of Determinants of Business Behavior and Neurolinguistic Programming

PETER LANG

Lausanne • Berlin • Bruxelles • Chennai • New York • Oxford

Library of Congress Cataloging-in-Publication Data
A CIP catalog record for this book has been applied for at the
Library of Congress.

**Bibliographic Information published by the
Deutsche Nationalbibliothek**
The Deutsche Nationalbibliothek lists this publication in the Deutsche
Nationalbibliografie; detailed bibliographic data is available online at
http://dnb.d-nb.de.

Authors:
prof. Ing. Dr. Róbert Štefko, Ph.D.; doc.PaedDr. Zuzana Birknerová, PhD., MBA;
PhDr. Anna Tomková, PhD.; Ing. Ivana Ondrijová, PhD.;
Mgr. Dávid Miško, PhD.; Mgr. Barbara Nicole Čigarská

Language proofreading and Editor:
Mgr. Hana Petrová

Reviewers:
prof. Daniel Meyer
University of Johannesburg, College of Business and Economics
prof. Sebastian Kot
Czestochowa University of Technology, Faculty of Management

The authors are responsible for the professional and linguistic aspects of this publication.

© prof. Ing. Dr. Róbert Štefko, Ph.D., doc.PaedDr. Zuzana Birknerová, PhD., MBA;
PhDr. Anna Tomková, PhD.; Ing. Ivana Ondrijová, PhD.;
Mgr. Dávid Miško, PhD.; Mgr. Barbara Nicole Čigarská

The publication was supported by the grant project VEGA No. 1/0428/23 Research of Subconscious Reactions of Customers Using Eye-Tracking and Other Tools Forming the Neuromarketing Instrumentarium.

ISBN 978-3-631-89786-7 (Print)
E-ISBN 978-3-631-89787-4 (E-PDF)
E-ISBN 978-3-631-89788-1 (E-PUB)
10.3726/b20600

© 2023 Peter Lang Group AG, Lausanne
Published by Peter Lang GmbH, Berlin, Deutschland

info@peterlang.com - www.peterlang.com

All parts of this publication are protected by copyright. Any
utilisation outside the strict limits of the copyright law, without
the permission of the publisher, is forbidden and liable to
prosecution. This applies in particular to reproductions,
translations, microfilming, and storage and processing in
electronic retrieval systems.

This publication has been peer reviewed.

Contents

Introduction 11

1 Business behavior 13
   1.1 Personality of businessman 13
   1.2 Purchasing and consumer behavior 16
   1.3 Negative factors of business behavior 19
   1.4 Business behavior and marketing 22

2 Marketing and sensory marketing 25
   2.1 Feeling versus perception 30
   2.2 Areas of sensory marketing 32
      2.2.1 Visual marketing 33
      2.2.2 Audio marketing 35
      2.2.3 Aroma marketing 37
      2.2.4 Haptic marketing 39
      2.2.5 Taste marketing 42

3 Neuromarketing 45
   3.1 Neuroscience 54
   3.2 Techniques in neuromarketing 56
      3.2.1 Functional Magnetic Resonance (fMRI) 56
      3.2.2 Electroencephalography (EEG) 57
      3.2.3 Magnetoencephalography (MEG) 57
      3.2.4 Computed Tomography (CT) 57
      3.2.5 Positron Emission Tomography (PET) 58
      3.2.6 Near-Infrared Spectroscopy (NIRS) 58
      3.2.7 Facial coding 58
      3.2.8 Facial Electromyography (EMG) 58
      3.2.9 Eye-tracking 58

Contents

    3.2.10 Measurement of physiological responses 59

  3.3 Neuromarketing in the context of the research 60

    3.3.1 Creation of trust 61

    3.3.2 Pricing strategy 61

    3.3.3 Negotiation 62

    3.3.4 Ethics 62

  3.4 Neuromarketing in selected sectors of marketing 63

    3.4.1 Neuromarketing and product design – *packaging* 65

    3.4.2 Neuromarketing and price – *pricing* 66

    3.4.3 Neuromarketing in advertisement 67

  3.5 Disadvantages of neuromarketing 68

4 Ethics of neuromarketing research 71

5 Neurolinguistic Programming (NLP) 75

  5.1 Neurological levels 78

    5.1.1 Surrounding 79

    5.1.2 Behavior 79

    5.1.3 Abilities and skills 79

    5.1.4 Values and beliefs 80

    5.1.5 Identity (mission) 80

    5.1.6 Connection (mission, transmission, meaning) 80

  5.2 Communication patterns based on NLP 81

    5.2.1 Mind reading 81

    5.2.2 Agreeable attitude 81

    5.2.3 A sequence of several affirmative statements or questions 81

    5.2.4 Hyptnotic accompanying and guidance 82

    5.2.5 Breaking the formula with NLP 82

    5.2.6 Reporting negative things 82

    5.2.7 The pattern of awareness in NLP 82

  5.3 NLP techniques 83

    5.3.1 Mind mapping 84

Contents

5.3.2 Brain gym 84
5.3.3 Disney's creative strategy 85
5.3.4 The six thinking hats model 86
5.3.5 NLP metaprograms 89
5.3.6 Reframing 90

6 Factors In NLP and business 93
6.1 Cognitive-emotional-behavioral factors in NLP 94
    6.1.1 Emotions as a mean of communication with the customer 94
    6.1.2 Emotions as a decision-making support 95
6.2 NLP as a tool of successful sales 97
6.3 Main principles of NLP in managerial practice and business 98
    6.3.1 Communication is continuous 98
    6.3.2 The meaning of communication is the reaction it generates 98
    6.3.3 People react to their idea and model of reality, not to reality itself 99
    6.3.4 Body, spirit, and soul are different, closely connected partial aspects of the whole person. Changing one part affects the others 99
    6.3.5 The most flexible person wins 99
    6.3.6 Unhappy, sick people are not broken – they use what they know and have, but in a way that doesn't satisfactorily meet their needs 100
    6.3.7 Everyone acts as best they can at the given moment 100
    6.3.8 Every behavior is valuable and useful in some context 100
    6.3.9 The more options a person can use to shape his life, the smoother and more satisfying his life will be 101
    6.3.10 Everyone is capable of achieving everything – in their own way 101
    6.3.11 Everyone has everything they need to handle life's problems – they just have to learn how to use it appropriately . 101
    6.3.12 There is no such a thing as failure, only results 101
    6.3.13 Problems taste better in smaller doses 101
    6.3.14 Behind every problematic behavior is a good intention 101
6.4 Pillars of NLP in practice 102

7 Research in the field of neuromarketing, business behavior and NLP 105

7.1 Sensory marketing research as an attribute of neuromarketing and business behavior 105

7.1.1 The aim and hypotheses of the first research project 105

7.1.2 Methodologies and methods of the first research project 106

7.1.3 Research sample of the first research project 107

7.1.4 Results of the first research project 108

7.1.5 Summary results of the first research project 113

7.2 Neuromarketing research and neurolinguistic programming 115

7.2.1 The aim and hypotheses of the second research project 115

7.2.2 Methodologies and methods of the second research project 116

NLP-C methodology (Neuro-Linguistic Programming – Communication) 117

NLP-T methodology (Neuro-Linguistic Programming – Techniques) 118

NM-SSP methodology (Neuromarketing – Shop, Seller, Product) 119

7.2.3 Research sample of the second research project 119

7.2.4 Results of the second research project 120

7.2.5 Summary results of the second research project 125

Conclusion 127

List of bibliographical references 131

SM-CEB
Sensory marketing – cognitions, emotions, behavior 151

DOBB – T
Determinants of business behavior – *trader* 153

Contents

DOBB – C
Determinants of business behavior – *customer* 157

The NLP Technique questionnaire (NLP-T) 161

The NLP Communication questionnaire (NLP-C) 163

The Neuromarketing questionnaire (NM-SSP) 165
Short paragraph about prof. Ing. Dr. Róbert Štefko, Ph.D. 167
Short paragraph about doc. PaedDr. Zuzana Birknerová, PhD., MBA 168
Short paragraph about PhDr. Anna Tomková, PhD. 168
Short paragraph about Ing. Ivana Ondrijová, PhD. 168
Short paragraph about Mgr. Dávid Miško, PhD. 169
Short paragraph about Mgr. Barbara Nicole Čigarská 169

Introduction

The monograph focuses on the conceptualization of sensory marketing and neurolinguistic programming as potential tools for implementing neuromarketing, as well as the evaluation of its feedback in relation to factors influencing business behavior.

The primary objective of the monograph is to clarify specific aspects of neuromarketing and neurolinguistic programming in the context of business behavior and to compare how subjectively businesspeople and customers perceive these aspects. The goal of the monograph is to clarify sensory marketing as an attribute of neuromarketing in business behavior and to determine factors that affect business behavior, neurolinguistic programming, and their utilization in that field.

In certain shopping situations, the store atmosphere has a more significant influence on the customer's decision than the product features or the price itself. The atmosphere may even have a direct impact on how customers develop attitudes about particular product categories. We perceive the atmosphere through our senses, which is how sensory marketing works. By introducing sensory stimulation into the sales environment, sensory marketing seeks to make customers feel good and, ideally, anticipate visiting a certain store in the future.

Development in the field of marketing research has reached a point where it is not sufficient to ask to find out the opinion and attitude of the customer. Researchers want to know what's going on in a customer's body while exposed to marketing stimuli, as well as how purchasing decisions he made. The use of medical devices to examine marketing activities created a new scientific field called neuromarketing. This interdisciplinary science has also enabled the development of sensory marketing, so today, it is possible to compare what customers say about themselves with what is happening in their bodies.

The monograph is dedicated to experts in the field of scientific research who engage in the study of neuromarketing and neurolinguistic programming in various contexts, especially in connection with sensory marketing in business behavior. The information which the monograph offers can be used by teachers who educate students in the field of neuromarketing, as well as by students who study the issues of marketing and business. The monograph is also intended for people who are interested in the issue of neurolinguistic programming and want to pay more attention to this issue and develop it in practice. Possibilities of using the presented methodologies, as well as theoretical and methodological knowledge, can be found in the preference of people for work, also in the education, coaching, and training of salespeople, employees, and people in general.

Authors

1 Business behavior

To assess sensory marketing as an attribute of neuromarketing in business behavior, and at the same time to assess the subjective perception of this issue from the perspective of traders and customers, it is necessary to explain fundamental, closely related concepts. Mainly, the concept of behavior needs to be clarified in general. Behavior is a way of expressing oneself in society, the way an individual behaves towards other people.

Business behavior stands for a theoretical definition of behavior in the field of business. Professional articles but also conceptual dictionaries contain different characteristics of a business. Viestová et al. (2006) offer a brief and concise trade definition. These authors define trade as the activity of exchanging services and goods via money. In the trade theory, the exchange of products is called buying and selling. Trade is a fundamental economic concept.

Szarková (2000) compares business to marketing in terms of the similarity of approaches, methods, and techniques used in it. The essential element is the contact between the trader and the customer. Business behavior is based on the essence of the concept of trade. It represents systems of behavior in the environment of business-sales relations. As with every behavior, business behavior depends on several variables, mostly self-confidence and the traits of the trader himself, and the cultural environment in the place of business also plays a role here (Graham et al., 2009).

Organizations have been dealing with the issue of business behavior since there is a competitive struggle between them. It is important to keep the best brand name for other business activities. The power of business behavior has the highest value in organizations, which they strive to improve and promote. Business behavior is the driving force of all organizations that try to analyze this process and, based on it, improve the attractiveness of their name and business (Birknerová et al., 2020).

Trading and business behavior depend on personal as well as cultural and social factors. Various factors are, to some extent, a prerequisite for the success of a businessman in building his business career.

1.1. Personality of businessman

Each person is unique and characterized by certain attributes of himself. Personality type can reveal how a person will react in life situations. Personality type is a set of qualities that occur together and are interconnected (Alexy, 2011). Human factors determine people's behavior and influence their interactions. Marketers not only determine strategy based on their own perspectives but also receive opinions from others. For a trader, it is important to be conscious of his abilities and skills and to be able to admit a mistake, ask for help, or reveal that he is capable to do something by himself (Yuan et al., 2017). Within sales management, salespeople are the most meaningful part of the company's function. The salesperson should be energetic, enthusiastic, persistent, proactive, self-confident, and devoted to his work. Selling means a certain way of life for the salesman. Furthermore, he should be independent, internally motivated, friendly, honest, hardworking, disciplined, enthusiastic, and should be able to build relationships with customers (Kotler, 2007).

Sales teams are also an important aspect of successful sales. Sales teams are a part of the marketing mix, which are very effective in achieving marketing goals and implementing marketing activities, such as finding and contacting new customers, sales, service, and gathering information. The high costs of sales teams require an effective sales management process. The company must proceed very carefully when choosing traders. When dealing with a customer, the marketer should be driven by a broader concept of relationship marketing. The relationship between the seller and the customer should be built on value and trust (Kotler, 2007). Regardless of the title, sales team members in modern organizations play a key role in the marketing mix. Sellers represent the only direct contact with the customer. Sales teams deal with wholesalers and retailers, seek support and help traders to sell products appropriately.

The profession of trader requires professional knowledge and communication skills. A professional trader can keep his boundaries while respecting the customer's boundaries in a way that he understands the customer's requirements and wishes related to the product and his needs. Building trust is a part of quality services. Empathy, product knowledge, and a trustworthy approach while the entire sales process are essential components of a professional trader (Sedláková, 2004).

Bělohlávek (2009) claims that every trader should have a personal vision. It is an active idea of the future state hence achieved results, position, or way of life. This vision guides him on his life path, helps him make decisions, and gives him the energy to work. Traders with a clear vision achieve significantly better results, whether at work or in personal life. According to Bedrnová and Nový (1998), the effective use of psychological knowledge enables the consolidation and creation of long-term business relationships so that both parties achieve the desired success. It is consequential to have knowledge about the personality of the trader, but also about the business activity itself and its process. It requires good interaction, communication, and also the application of psychological knowledge during the sale.

In today's modern age, using psychological knowledge and methods helps traders to resolve conflicts in the work environment. It is confirmed that in order to achieve the required work success, it is significant to get to know the person as such and his mental health. Quality employees form the basis of a successful company. Psychological knowledge and procedures are used by companies not only in the sale of products but also in the selection of the right employees (Szarková, 2007). According to Armstrong (1999), a businessman who wants to manage a company successfully should have quality personality traits which include regulating behavior and emotions, the ability to solve problems and take responsibility for them, making the right decisions in critical situations, finding the best solution, assertiveness, effort to promote the organization and its products and insist on professional opinion. For a trader to be successful, he must use various interpersonal skills in his work.

According to Bedrnová and Nový (1998), one of the qualities that helps traders succeed is extraversion. It is characterized by openness, sociability, interest in communication with people, adaptability, and networking. Compared to introverts, who are more focused on privacy and timid in making contacts, extroverts have a better chance of finding a job in this business. Ambition, perseverance, and responsibility are also essential. Openness and fairness help to build trust between the trader and another party in the business.

Mišík (2016) states internal qualities, which to a certain extent affect the success of traders. The author declares that the profession of trader is one of the most difficult and to become a trader, one must have certain preconditions. These affect sales success. Emotional intelligence, business and communication skills, and expertise could be learned over a lifetime, but self-organization the trader either has or does not have. Emotional intelligence describes a condition in which a good salesperson must be able to control his emotions and at the same time, manage the emotions of customers. The fear of rejection must go beyond perception. Emotional intelligence also includes inner motivation, values, and attitudes.

Pendleton (2012) states that emotionally unstable individuals do not achieve job satisfaction. Šuleř (2008) claims that emotional lability takes various forms, such as excessive cautiousness, or slight agitation, which means less chance of success. Business and communication skills are required for impeccable knowledge of sales techniques, but even this does not ensure 100 % success. Charisma and an optimistic attitude are also needed. Some people are already born with these abilities. Business skills can also be acquired throughout life and can be trained. Expertise is important so that the seller knows not only the product but also the market in which he operates. This quality is probably the most straightforward because it is about obtaining and processing information. The trader may not have the skills to know this, it is a practical matter. This quality can be influenced, but it is more about the personality of the trader. Not everyone can reconcile work responsibilities within a schedule, and this is also reflected in work results.

According to Farley (2020), quality business skills are essential elements in the search for long-term success. No books can change a trader if he has mental obstacles that undermine his efforts from the very beginning. Quality traders have common psychological qualities that improve their personal strength and ability to achieve results and cope with difficult and stressful situations.

Of course, the fundamental skills of a trader include communication. Khelerová (2010) lists active listening, questioning techniques, nonverbal communication, empathy, and removing barriers as the most important. Active listening can also have traps, such as inattentive listening, haste, jumping into speech, passivity, and hypersensitivity. This manifestation should be avoided by the trader. The one who actively listens has a better opportunity to get to know the customer and design the product exactly according to his ideas.

Knowledge of psychology is required when establishing relationships with customers. Many traders use it unknowingly and automatically, but more successful are those who have knowledge in this area. According to Limbeck (2012), it is better to try one, at most two psychological patterns on many clients and become a professional in them, than try different psychological practices on each client and give a bad impression of one's own ignorance. An experienced trader can obtain information about the customer, which he can process and use to his advantage.

1.2 Purchasing and consumer behavior

We become a customer at the moment when we show interest in a service or product. By fulfilling the needs by purchasing a product, we get into the position of a buyer. The buyer does not automatically become the final user (end-user) as he may buy products for his family (Zamazalová, 2009).

The author summarized the differences between the following terms:

(a) a customer – expresses interest in purchasing the product,
(b) a buyer – the customer at the time of purchase of the product,

(c) a consumer – the end-user of the product (products or services are consumed, i.e., they did not necessarily have to buy them).

The legal definition of the consumer can be found in Act no. 250/2007 on consumer protection and it is a natural person (non-entrepreneur) who does not act within the subject of his business activity, employment, or profession when completing and fulfilling a consumer contract. At first glance, it may seem that there is no difference between a consumer and a customer. The opposite is true. In the sense of the Consumer Protection Act, a consumer is not an entrepreneur, nor he is a customer who buys goods for his work or profession. Such a customer who is not a consumer cannot legally exercise his rights under the above-mentioned consumer protection laws. The Slovak legislation is aware of the legal exception, where the entrepreneur is also a consumer if he acts to provide services of general interest, promote a public benefit purpose, or fulfilling the public benefit intent.

A consumer is an individual that enters the market intending to purchase goods and services to meet his needs. When buying, he spends money, which is a simple tool for measuring expenses. The consumer's goal is to maximize utility (Lisý et al., 2005). The concept of a consumer is broader and includes everything that a person consumes, even what he does not buy by himself. The customer is the one who orders, buys, and pays for the goods or services. The paying customer does not have to be necessarily a consumer, it is the end-user of the product or service (Vysekalová, 2011).

Andrejkovič (2007) defines a customer as anyone who enters the store, even if he does not make a purchase. The buyer is then defined as the person who buys the goods or services and consumes them. He understands the consumer as a broader term, which refers to the final consumer of the goods or services, regardless of whether he made the purchase by himself or received the goods as a gift. Since the term customer is narrower than the term consumer and it is the person who buys products and services, in his case we are talking about shopping behavior. On the other hand, a consumer is a person who uses those services and products after purchase but does not necessarily buy them (Zamazalová, 2009).

To be able to provide products that meet the needs of customers, traders must first understand their usual behavior. We also refer to this behavior as shopping behavior. In today's modern and technologically rapidly evolving time, it is relatively challenging to offer quality products and services from traders to keep up with customers. Last but not least, to understand customer behavior, we must also start from the context of consumer behavior. We consider shopping behavior to be one of the phases of consumer behavior (Zamazalová, 2009).

Opinions on shopping behavior vary. Schiffman and Kanuk (2004) define shopping behavior as a consumer activity – finding, buying, using, evaluating goods and services from which he expects to meet needs. According to Vasiľová, Dražová (2015), we can characterize shopping behavior as choosing how the consumer manages his resources, time, effort, and financial resources in choosing products he eventually prefers to satisfy his needs.

Based on the above, the consumer gets into a certain position, which affects the buying situation (Schiffman, Kanuk, 2004):

- the consumer as the initiator who gives the first impulse to purchase a particular product,
- the consumer as an influencer who influences others based on his own opinion, whether or not to purchase the product,
- the consumer as the decisive person who says what, how, and when to buy,
- the consumer as the buyer who buys the product and consumes it at the same time.

According to Kotler and Keller (2013), consumer behavior refers to the decision-making processes involved in selecting, acquiring, utilizing, and discarding goods and services that meet the requirements and preferences of the consumer at a particular moment. According to the AMA (American Marketing Association), consumer behavior is defined as the dynamic interactions between individuals and their surroundings to satisfy demands, which include emotions, knowledge, and behavior (Bennett, 1995).

Táborecká-Petrovičová (2011) defines consumer behavior as social and mental processes that take place just before purchase (awareness of the need, obtaining information, evaluation of alternatives, selection of alternatives), during the purchase (purchasing behavior) and after the purchase (post-purchase evaluation of usefulness, comparison of expected facts, satisfaction or dissatisfaction, awareness of cognitive dissonance, consumption process, handling of the product and disposal of the product). Shopping behavior is sometimes irrational and incomprehensible to traders.

To understand shopping behavior, neuromarketing – a new interdisciplinary approach helps traders and marketers. Marketers use sensory marketing to positively influence because already in the first phase of perception the stimuli are transferred to the customer's senses, which they can successfully stimulate by using appropriate tools and consequently influence customers' shopping behavior (Vysekalová, 2011).

1.3 Negative factors of business behavior

Negative factors of business behavior may include unfair business practices, aggressive behavior, and manipulation. The use of an assertive reaction is an appropriate response and defense against such business behavior.

In the market of traders offering products, we quite often encounter two main problems, which are negatively evaluated from an ethical point of view (Bárta et al., 2009):

- an attempt by traders to take the advantage of unfair commercial practices, deceptive manners or omission,
- an aggressive business practice uses harassment, coercion, including the use of physical force, or excessive influence that leads to its irrational behavior.

Misleading trader's behavior causes or may cause the customer to decide on a business transaction that he would not otherwise make because it contains incorrect information and is therefore untrue, or in any way misleads the average customer, even if is this information is factually correct, in relation to (Bárta et al., 2009):

(a) the product – its existence and nature,
(b) the characteristics of the product – for example, its composition, origin, design, the purpose of use, possibilities of use, etc.,
(c) prices,
(d) the right to exchange or refund money,
(e) marketing, including comparative advertising, which creates a possibility of confusion with any other product, trademark, trademark, or other sign and the like.

The misleading omission of procedure by the trader consists in hiding essential information about the product or providing it in an unclear, incomprehensible, multi-meaningful, or inappropriate manner (Consumer Protection Act).

To defend against misleading and other negative behavior from the trader, it is important to react assertively. Assertive business behavior is based on the assumption that it is possible to acquire abilities, skills, and techniques that help to overcome the effects of emotions. Assertiveness allows control own actions and helps to maintain self-esteem (Lahnerová, 2012).

With assertiveness, we realize our values as well as the values of others. The opposite of assertiveness in business is a manifestation of superiority, arrogance, and manipulation. Assertive manifestations are manifestations in an authentic form, without stylization, manipulation, and embellishment, and the assertive individual shows a positive attitude towards others (Lelková, 2015).

In the field of business behavior, assertive communication skills are important for a successful trader. The basis of assertive behavior according to Lelková (2014) is:

- straightforward phrasing of objectives,
- open and direct communication,
- the ability to show an understanding of the other party's views,
- the ability not to make concessions on essential matters and to act flexibly where appropriate.

Through assertive behavior, we are aware of our actions, responsible for the actions, and have them under control. We can decide what we want to get from a certain situation, so we set goals, understand and perceive other's feelings, needs, and attitudes, understand what we want to get from a given situation, and look for a mutual and acceptable solution through open and direct communication (Lelková, 2014).

Assertive behavior should be used especially in managing workplace conflicts, leading and motivating people, speaking at workshops, providing and receiving feedback, in negotiations, and whenever it is not possible to give space to negative feelings. Another area of interest in business behavior appears to be engagement, which means behavior that positively affects the overall results of the company and is influenced by the character and personality of each individual. Engaged traders are those who show enthusiasm and devotion to their work. Engagement in business behavior is related to their assertive approach, which is characterized by awareness, which will be ultimately appreciated by customers via repeated purchases and good references (Lelková, 2014).

The opposite of assertive behavior is aggression, manipulative behavior, or passive behavior. By aggressive behavior, traders try to cover up their uncertainty, and fear of the result of an unknown environment. Aggression is accompanied by expressions such as anger, bitterness, and the like. The factor that contributes to aggression is stress and a lifestyle that minimizes physical exertion. Engaged behavior and stress are interrelated while the main cause of negative behavior as a result of stress is the excessive involvement of the trader, who is trying to be excessively communicative. The combination of these two determinants appears to be an extreme form of behavior. Manipulative behavior from traders includes withholding information, flattery, blackmail, avoiding answers, distraction, trivialization, unwillingness to understand, the use of false arguments, and the like. Traders fight for the interest and appreciation of their customers in all sorts of ways. To manipulate customers, traders use various tricks, including psychological tricks, through which they try to attract consumers in a targeted way and thus influence their purchasing decisions (Lelková, 2014).

The style of manipulation depends on the type of personality. Some choose manipulation based on simulated helplessness, others choose an aggressive style. Lahnerová (2009) divides components of manipulation into nine characteristic personality styles:

1. *A dictator* – refers to the authorities, traditions, and references of ancestors; we are meeting with him in the position of authoritative boss in the company; his reactions do not stand up to opposition.
2. *Poor man* – thanks to his frequent and loudly emphasized handicaps; he creates the impression that he would be extremely happy to do this or that, but because he does not have enough strength, he often stays in the story; the act must be made by someone else; he is willing to diminish his abilities, but in reality, he is covering up his laziness or unwillingness.
3. *Cagey* – he estimates what is the best for him quickly; he simply forgets or suddenly becomes uncomfortable with discomfiting tasks; he has no high ambitions and performs only simple tasks.
4. *Ivy* – he smirks around others in some way that emphasizes his dependence on them; he allows stronger co-workers to take care of him; there does not exist the except for the hint of emotional blackmail.
5. *Rough* – uses a certain physical strength and superiority in a team, uses rude behavior to control co-workers, and in extreme cases begins to swear or use vulgarism and threats; he knows no discussion or compromise.
6. *Sacrifice* – often occurs in intergenerational conflict, among co-workers evokes feelings of guilt, the impression that they are evil and characterless.
7. *The last righteous* – he constantly evokes feelings of guilt and inadequacy in the work team, but he considers himself to be faultless; he emphasizes that he performs the assigned tasks best.
8. *Guardian* – protects chosen ones from the team from all pitfalls; he still cares about them, but often forgets to ask them if they are interested in it; he is convinced that he knows best what is good for others, he does not even allow another option.
9. *Mobster* – violently manipulates; he does not get dirty his hands by himself, he has people for that; he offers some protection but does not ask if a team member is interested in it.

Manipulation is one of the unpleasant and dangerous strategies in the field of interpersonal communication. It disrupts the symmetry of relationships, minimizing the possibility of agreement and creative cooperation between colleagues in the team. The space for the growth of teamwork, interpersonal connections, and corporate strategy is restricted if manipulation starts to be used frequently as a means of communication in the workplace. On a verbal or nonverbal level, manipulation is achievable via conscious and unconscious techniques (Birknerová et al., 2013).

Another negative behavior that is the opposite of assertive behavior is passive behavior, which embodies the denial of one's own rights. Passive behavior is characterized by body language, specifically lowered eyes, justifying phrases, acceptance of guilt, use of submissive expressions, and the like. It is based on the belief that the needs of others are always a priority (Lahnerová, 2009).

From the aforementioned, it follows that business behavior can vary, and this can include unethical commercial actions by entrepreneurs (traders) toward clients. Marketing theory and practice are intertwined with knowledge of business behavior.

1.4 Business behavior and marketing

Every behavior represents the way a person acts outside of society, that is, how he treats other people. Behavior is conditioned by a range of predictors that lead to some outcome in behavior, whether prosocial, ethical, or unwanted unethical behavior. The following paragraphs are devoted to the theoretical nature of marketing and business behavior, which is related to the creation of relationships between the trader and customers, within mutual contact (Kovaľová, Birknerová, 2018).

Marketing is a scientific discipline that emphasizes the information, strategic and operational interconnection of the company and its surroundings. Its essence lies in respecting the wishes of the consumer. Marketing provides knowledge on how to initiate, facilitate and execute market transactions. The mission of marketing is education, management practice, and support in the integration of the company into the educational system (Kita et al., 2010).

Kotler and Armstrong (2004) state that marketing is more than any other goal-oriented tool for customers. Probably the simplest definition is that marketing is the management of customer relationships in order to make a profit. The dual goal of marketing is to attract new customers by promising higher values and maintaining existing customers by providing them with the satisfaction of their needs.

According to Dudinska et al. (2000), the essence of all definitions of marketing creates common elements and it is, the fact that it is a complex process, not just a fragmented set of individual activities, trying to understand the problems of customers and based on that offers them solutions to these problems. The classic model of how marketing works as a process is that the initial phase of this process is to estimate needs and create the idea of products that should satisfy them. The whole process is completed by the satisfaction of customer needs and customer satisfaction itself is visible in sales at a profit, which is the main goal and attribute of a successful business.

Currently, mass marketing has taken the position of promoting individualized customer relationships (Bartáková, 2015):

- emphasis on the individual (customer),
- long-term customer / trader relationship,
- emphasis on the psychological factors involved in the sales processes (personality factors, environmental factors, psychological characteristics of the product, the relational components of the sales process itself).

We include personal sales and direct marketing among direct communication tools. The role of traders is to convince current and potential customers. The success of a company depends on sales as an interpersonal part of the communication mix. Salespeople need to master direct marketing and the process of forming individual contact with customers to build strong individual relationships. The trader's direct contact with the customer receives an immediate response from the customer. Then companies are able to store and create databases about customers and their opinions, which is very important in the future for the functioning of the company (Kotler, 2007). Direct marketing is also beneficial for customers and is convenient, as the buyer has direct and immediate access to information and products, either at home or directly at the store. The author distinguishes the following forms of direct marketing:

- personal sale,
- mobile marketing,
- consignment catalogs,
- online marketing.

Communication at the place of sale, as well as in other forms of sales, is very important for influencing the shopping behavior on the part of traders, as the trader is always focused on the target group of customers and the nature of the offered product or service. The place of sale is a very important marketing tool that marketers must use to create the need for customers to buy their brand. A place of sale with countless scents, colors, sounds, and products offers the widest interaction with the customer, who perceives it with all his senses (Krishna, 2010).

Marketing that is applied at the point of sale is called in-store marketing. For the optimal functioning of in-store marketing, it is important to create communication (POP communication) between a distributor who is interested in promoting their product and a trader. When making a purchase, the environment in which the sale takes place matters. In the event of a personal sale, the trader's approach can have an impact on the process' outcome just like the product. In the personal approach of the trader towards the customer, it is possible to psychologically analyze and determine certain stable factors: *sales situations*. A specific good or service is at the top, and at the bottom are a trader and a customer who learns about the offer through the trader.

According to Komárková et al. (1993), these factors appear to have ideal relationships if:

- there are positive relations between the trader and the goods,
- the trader has an excellent knowledge of the product,
- there is a mutually positive relationship between the trader and the customer,
- the trader has a good knowledge of the needs and interests of the customer and is able to adapt the offer to these needs,
- a good relationship between the customer and the trader can positively affect the customer's relationship with the goods,
- there is a positive attitude of the customer to the goods, which leads from the purchase intention to the purchase decision.

The field of marketing has undergone the necessary innovation in recent years. It is a continuous and long-term activity consisting in satisfying the needs of customers in the form of various tools and the use of various marketing principles, which are the basis of managerial decisions. Marketing research allows us to take measures that meet the current time and customer requirements. Improvement of in-store marketing through sensory marketing is currently garnering increasing attention.

2 Marketing and sensory marketing

The word marketing comes from the English word market – market, where the suffix -ing means the expression of a certain event, a certain activity that is constantly performed on the market. The term "marketing" became well-known in our nation through time and is now frequently employed. But it's not usually understood and explained correctly. It is possible to meet the constraint of this concept at the level of sales (physical distribution), or it is associated only with advertising or promotional activities of the company. However, marketing is a broader concept (Kita et al., 2005).

In the professional literature are several definitions and characteristics of the term marketing. The main task of marketing is to attract customers and retain them. In addition, it highlights the fact that marketing affects the entire company and not just those working in the marketing department. Despite minor differences, all definitions of marketing share the following theme: *customer orientated*. It is the basic principle of marketing. Consequently, the core of the approach is the knowledge of the customer. In the existing market conditions, none of the companies has automatically guaranteed sales of products, but foremost, it has to attract the customer by preparing an offer (product, price, method of sale, and communication) that meets his needs and wishes, which means that it will bring to him expected benefits. Simply said, a business must determine whether customers are even remotely interested in the product and whether it will actually sell before it begins to produce and sell it. Only then it is probable to succeed in the market and achieve goals. Additionally, marketing should assist the organization in reducing business risk and failure risk (Srpová, 2010).

Nowadays, there are numerous definitions and ideas presented in professional literature, making it difficult to identify the one that would be applicable to all societies and circumstances. Since the term was first used in America, we suppose that we can cite the statutes of the American Marketing Society (AMA), which describe marketing as a process of planning and practical performance of development concept, price formation, and production stimulation, sorting of ideas, products, and services in order to form mutual relations that satisfy individual and social needs (Horáková, 1995). In the early 1950s of the past century, this idea received attention in Europe.

According to marketing expert Kotler (1995), marketing is managerial and social process by which individuals and groups obtain what they demand and need by creating, offering, or changing products with others. It represents a company's increased marketing ability, which could potentially lead to a new era of high economic growth and raising their standard of living.

There does not exist generally accepted definition of marketing that captures the specific nature of the marketing application in different types of organizations and markets and at dissimilar stages of market development. Renowned authors have created several custom definitions. According to Kotler and Armstrong (2007), marketing is a managing process wherein people and groups create, sell, and provide valuable things in order to satisfy their wants and needs. Planning, implementing, pricing, promoting, and dispersing ideas and products are all steps in the process of bringing about improvements that will please both individuals and organizations. In his book, Kretter (2007) describes marketing as a sophisticated corporate philosophy.

Marketing is a set of activities and processes that should identify or develop a customer's need or desire for a related product, communicate, and then distribute that product to the customer. The result is a mutually beneficial exchange, which leads to long-term customer satisfaction and the satisfaction of the organization and society (Richterová, 1993).

Many years of development in marketing have made it impossible for certain companies to use specific rules and standards when using it. Accordingly, marketing is a set of different activities that differ, and mutual uniform use depends on the product or service we want to sell and the nature of the market where we want to implement the product (Trebuňa, 2007).

The broad definition of marketing in the global economy requires ongoing revisions to the usage guidelines for marketing. The most recent definition of marketing, for instance, states that it is an activity, a collection of institutions, and a set of procedures for developing, supplying, and altering requirements with value for consumers, clients, partners, and the general public. New definitions also come up with new forms of marketing (Denton, 2018).

Regarding the older definitions, this definition reflects the transformation in marketing from the supply of services to more general values, as well as the evolution from the consumer to all market participants, including society as a whole. As part of marketing activities, greater emphasis is placed on marketing communication involving sponsorship, sales promotion, direct marketing, advertising, and digital marketing communication. Kotler (1995) talks about three meanings of marketing:

- overall management philosophy,
- one of the management functions of the company,

- includes all business activities and techniques that are part of the movement of goods and services from the manufacturer to the customer.

Many people think of marketing as just sales and advertising, but these are just two marketing features that are often not even the most important. Contemporary marketing should be comprehended, above all, as a fulfillment of customers' needs. Sales occur after the product is manufactured, but marketing begins long before that. A good trader must find out what the market needs and decide if there is an opportunity. Marketing then continues throughout the product life cycle. The primary task is to attract new customers and keep them long-lasting by innovating the product, learning from the results, or trying to repeat the success (Dorčák, Pollák, 2010).

Based on given marketing definitions, it is possible to state that with the help of purposeful management of marketing processes, the company tries to achieve a level of demand that allows it to meet its corporate goals. From the above, it is possible to conclude that marketing management stands for the management of demands in many companies. Dudinská et al. (2000) state that part of the marketing mission is also the creation of communication programs that transform needs and wishes into a demand that waits to be satisfied.

The priority on which marketing assembles is human needs. These can be defined as a feeling of lack, which includes basic physical needs, social and individual needs, including the desire for knowledge, and self-realization. Human wants represent human needs shaped by the external culture and personality of the individual. People have restrained needs, but their desires have no limits, only the resources to fulfill them. Therefore, people choose products that will bring them the most benefit and satisfaction for their money. Therefore, it is conceivable to claim that people's desires become demands as long as they are able and willing to pay for the offered good. For the creation of marketing strategies, a comprehensive insight of client wants, wishes, and demand is essential (Dudinská et al., 2006).

Today, all successful businesses share a strong commitment to marketing and customer service. These businesses concentrate on fulfilling consumers' requests in narrowly defined target markets. They inspire employees to offer clients excellence and high value, resulting in high customer satisfaction. Marketing is primarily about customers, who are an integral part of the marketing system. The value creation for the customer and his satisfaction is the heart of modern marketing. The main goal of marketing is to attract new customers by promising higher value and retaining them by satisfying their needs (Ferrel, Hartline, 2010).

A person's interactions with physical and social settings, as well as physical states, are all directly influenced by sensory inputs. They play a crucial role in all facets of life, especially the consumer world. The field of sensory marketing has developed in an attempt to understand how consumers' emotions, perceptions, memories, choices and preferences are influenced by their senses, with the intention of more effective managing of them (Aydınoğlu, Sayın, 2016). Products are sensual in their character (relating to feelings or senses), and the more companies can emphasize or create the sensuality of products, the more attractive those products are to consumers (Krishna, 2010).

Throughout the day, customers are exposed to hundreds of marketing messages and items. Choice processes for consuming become increasingly difficult as a result of the abundance of information and possibilities. Additionally, the market exhibits a high degree of brand parity, in which several goods offer comparable (if not identical) functional advantages (Muncy, 1996). Customers no longer purchase things just for their pragmatic and monetary value, but rather for the experience features offered by businesses (Schmitt, 1999). Firms strive to create a positive and differentiated total consumer experience by combining the emotive, experiential, symbolic, sensory, and functional qualities of their products in order to prevent brand parity (Haeckel et al., 2003). Randhir et al. (2016) define sensory marketing as a tool for measuring and clarifying customer emotions, but they also see it as a way to capitalize on new market possibilities to assure the product's long-term success.

According to Nízka (2007), it is critical to impact all senses in such a manner that the product or service is seen differently from competitive products and services, hence creating the brand's and product's psychological competitive advantage at the market. The major goal of sensory marketing, according to Krishna (2011), is to measure how customers' senses impact purchase behavior and how much they affect decision-making.

Customer experience is a mixture of product experience (product interaction; Hoch 2002), brand experience (interaction with brand-related stimuli, such as colors, shapes, and fonts; Brakus et al., 2009), consumer experience (product consumption and use), and purchasing experience (interaction with the retail environment, retailers, and other customers; Hui, Bateson, 1991). Customer experience includes and combines a cognitive dimension relating to a sensory dimension referring to sensory incentives provided by the brand, an affective dimension relating to brand-generated feelings, behavioral dimension relating to consumer interaction with a brand, product's ability to evoke brand thinking in the consumer (Zarantonello, Schmitt, 2010).

Many brands use a combination of symbolic, sensory and functional values in marketing communication. Consequently, incorporating additional sensory cues into the overall customer experience (sensory marketing) has become widespread in managers' efforts to provide greater and unique value to their customers (Aydınoğlu, Sayın, 2016).

Sensory stimuli are building blocks of perception processes and are directly linked to customers' emotions and knowledge. Connecting with customers via sensory cues helps marketers to enrich and manage the overall customer experience. Consequently, there is a growing need to understand the effects of perceptions and sensory cues on customers during their purchase, inquiry, consumption or post-consumption (Brakus et al., 2008).

Sensory marketing provides customers with a multi-sensory experience with the intention of creating additional value. The whole consumer experience is shaped by the sensory elements of products and the marketing environment (taste, sound, smell, touch or look), either separately or in combination. The basis of perceptual processes is formed by the olfactory, auditory, haptic, gustatory, and visual aspects of marketing stimuli, which can also increase affect and excitement about the experience (Aydınoğlu, Sayın, 2016). Krishna (2010) defines sensory marketing as marketing that engages consumers' senses and influences their perceptions, judgments, and behaviors. Sensory marketing provides stimuli that evoke sensations and then investigates how individuals perceive them and how physical sensations influence their judgments and behavior. Many items have many qualities that appeal to one or more senses. When a buyer decides to buy a birthday cake, the way the cake is displayed (on a tray or in a paper box), the design and colors of the cake, its scent, the retail atmosphere, the seller's decision, words and tone of voice, all affect and create a completely different shopping experience. Contextual details such as store lighting and colors, ceiling height, carpeted or not carpeted floor, salesperson height and weight, etc., can also contribute to the overall experience.

The customer experience is holistic, linking the consumer's view of the product to every other element of the surrounding environment. Customers gain from this experience because it satisfies a variety of their wants. The overall experience satisfies the customer's desire to purchase a birthday cake (functional need), as well as his need for self-actualization and/or social fulfillment (symbolic need), while satisfying sensory demands (experiential need) (Park et al., 1986).

The consumer's overall sensory experience will have an impact (consciously or unconsciously) on how they judge the cake and all subsequent behavioral outcomes. These impacts are typically modest, which increases their potency.

Customers do not necessarily reject them because they do not perceive them as apparent marketing messages (Aydınoğlu, Sayın, 2016).

Currently, sensory marketing is the most successful method for influencing a customer's shopping-related emotions. Sensory marketing keeps track of the emotions that influence customers' decisions to buy things. Even before the buyer buys the product itself, it aims to wow all of their senses through actions centered on items, distribution, communication (Boček et al., 2009).

Senses help a person to learn about the world around him from birth and accompany him throughout his life. That is why they can be simple and at the same time, effective in influencing human behavior.

2.1 Feeling versus perception

Perception and sensation are stages of sensory processing. Perception is the awareness or understanding of sensory information. Sensation happens when a stimulus hits the receptor cells of a sense organ – it is biochemical (and neurological) in nature. A simple way to understand the difference between perception and sensation are visual illusions. The one is displayed below (see Figure 2.1 for the cafe wall illusion). In the cafe wall illusion, the horizontal lines are parallel, which means the biochemical sensation of the light falling on the eyes are horizontal; but, the perception is that they are not horizontal – after the brain interprets sensations, the lines no longer appear parallel. Over time, we learned to expect things to bend (like wooden planks) when a block (like a brick) is placed on top of them. Therefore, the lines with the blocks on top do not appear parallel. There exkst hundreds of similar visual illusions (Krishna, 2012).

Figure 2.1. Café wall illusion
(*Source:* Krishna, 2012)

Not just the sense of sight may differentiate between feeling and perception, but other senses as well. Recognition of speech is another sense. Japanese adults are unable to distinguish between L and R, while newborns can. Japanese adults have learned not to tell the difference since their language doesn't matter. Although an audio signal (sensation) may carry both an L and an R sound, the brain will interpret both as L (perception) – by the Japanese will be heard both sounds as L (Wolfe et al., 2006).

Again, perceptions and feelings are largely beyond our control and different. Japanese adults can train to hear L and R as distinguishable, but proactive training is required to mind the difference (Krishna, 2012).

Analogies to personalities frequently center on haptic traits. The significance of interacting with customers and their products cannot be overstated. In the 4th century BC, Aristotle presented the theory of aesthetic sensations, which suggests that our five senses are arranged hierarchically, with tactile (tactual) at the top and the other senses increasing the sharpness of touch. According to Aristotle, touch delivers an authentic picture of an object's inner character, which is why a kitten's silky fur would reflect its natural gentleness of character. Touch and the cosmos were also linked since sexual stimulation operated through the touch, allowing to humanity to thrive (Krishna, 2012).

Peck and Childers (2003) created the Need-for-Touchscale, which captures individual differences in the need for touch. The scale consists of two subscales: autotelic and instrumental. As the name suggests, the instrumental need for touch is functionality, i.e., for a particular goal, generally to buy the product. A typical sentence for the scale is: The single way to be assured that a product is worth purchasing is to actually touch it. On the other hand, the autotelic need for touch captures the uncontrollable touch or emotional component of touch (the touch just for the sake of touch). A standard sentence is: Touching of products may be enjoyable. The functional and the pleasure dimensiona have six questions (sentences). The scale is widely used and able to distinguish differences in judgments based on differences in the urge for touch (Krishna, Morrin, 2008).

People touching products, people touching people, and products contacting products are all affected by such disparities. Scent and memory research has been undertaken in the fundamental sciences, psychology, and, more recently, marketing. This study offers various biological or anatomical (structural) reasons why fragrance-encoded information can endure longer than information encoded by other sensory inputs. Among them include the physical and neurological closeness of systems connected with fragrance and memory. The limbic system, which comprises the olfactory bulb, amygdala, and hippocampus, is distinguished by rapid synaptic communications among its elements (Herz and Engen 1996).

Only two synapses connect the olfactory nerve to the amygdala, which is well known for its purpose in emotion and a significant part in defining emotional memory (Cahill et al., 1995).

The hippocampus is even more concerned in memory than the amygdala (Eichenbaum, 1996). Since there are three synapses between the olfactory nerve and the hippocampus, this interaction is extremely strong. Therefore, the transmission of olfactory information is different from the transmission of other senses, none of which has such a straight connection with memory.

There is research on the ability of scents, compared to stimuli from other sensory modalities, to evoke memories of autobiographical or memories of events that happened long ago. Herz (2004) stated that memories evoked by olfactory alerts were more emotional than those with other types of stimuli.

Lwin, Morrin, and Krishna (2010) enhance a Dual Coding Theory in memory research beyond the typical focus on visual and verbal information to include olfactory information. They control the absence or presence of olfactory stimuli (scent) and visual stimuli and assess the effect on verbal appeal. They discovered that scent improves verbal knowledge memory and that smell-based retrieval signals improve the facilitative impact of visuals on recall. These two olfactory effects have been found to occur in both encoding and retrieval and occur after a time delay (i.e., the scent is a memory booster after a time delay). They underline that a scent-enhanced memory is susceptible to retrospective interference (from later recovered information), and that lost knowledge can be restored by scent-based retrieval stimuli.

When we hear the tone of words, we attribute meaning to it and even distinguish the physical features of the the sound's source – whether it is animate (person, dog, or cat) or inanimate (cell phone, car). A high-frequency bark, for example, is linked with a little dog, but a deep, low-frequency growl is connected with a massive, ferocious-looking dog. Similarly, "Macho" males are supposed to have stronger voices, drive expensive automobiles, and close doors with smoother low-frequency noises (Krishna, 2012).

2.2 Areas of sensory marketing

Boček, Jesenský, and Krofiánová (2009) describe in their book sensory marketing as one of the marketing disciplines. The primary goal is to trigger customers to purchase, strengthen their relationship with goods, and focus on all their senses. European specialist in sensory communication Bruno Dance believes that for a period, the goal of marketers in sensory marketing was the amount by which their turnover increased. Today, things are different, and for marketers buying items, it's critical to establish a connection with the customer.

The senses the individual possesses have an impact on learning about his surroundings and building his own reality. Sight, hearing, aroma, touch, and taste are planned to protect a person from a potential threat or danger. With the assistance of these senses, it is simpler to evaluate scenarios in which they engage with a specific service or product, therefore they also have a new meaning in this context, in the context of the marketing environment.

2.2.1. Visual marketing

Dani and Pabalkar (2013) consider vision to be the strongest of all five senses, as up to 80 % of information is obtained through it. The association between the eyes and the brain is fast. Humans only need 45 milliseconds to identify an object by sight.

Visual marketing still has an irreplaceable place in the customer's purchasing decision. Sensory marketing does not try to replace visual communication, but for effective stimulation of emotions, the use or combination of more sensory marketing is appropriate. Visual marketing works with colors, light, graphics, placement of goods, and the overall effect and appearance of the store space and the appearance of salespeople. The color of the environment has physical, economic and psychological effect on the customer and causes different reactions. The psychology of colors is very important in marketing communication (Vysekalová, 2012).

We visually perceive up to 80 % of the stimuli around us. Visual effects are reproduced by means of modern technology in the form of large-scale indicators. Vysekalová (2012) describes visual marketing as working with graphics, light, colors, and following an array of products on shelves or placement in the store, but also how employees dress. The use of warm and cold tones, as well as the way of perceiving colors, is still traditional. It is the psychology of colors, the author of which is J. W. Goethe. This perception of colors is dependent on its symbolism, e.g., black color in most areas means sadness, death, evil, and white color, on the contrary, goodness, purity, and cheerfulness. Next, we could continue with the color red, which is usually associated with the strength of a person or is often associated with falling in love, love, and romance. Correct lighting selection and how it affects the saturation of the chosen colors are also crucial factors in this color decision.

The sight allows individuals to discover what is happening around and it is considered to be the most dominant sense when perceiving services or goods (Hultén, 2011). Consumer perception is influenced by brand-related cues such as distinctive colors (Meyers-Levy, Peracchio, 1995), shapes (Veryzer, Hutchinson, 1998), and background design elements (Mandel, Johnson, 2002) influence consumer perception of the brand in a context that is ready for them. As previously mentioned, brand-related stimuli can also appear as part of the environment where the product is sold or displayed (Brakus et al., 2009). The whole consumer experience is also influenced by a corporate website, a shop, or print or television advertisements. Visual lines such as the layout, decoration, size, lighting and colors of the store, or visual aspects of product packaging, influence perception of the consumer and consumption decisions (Aydınoğlu, Sayın, 2016). Bias in Visual perception is important in the field of consumer behavior because it affects judgments about product size and consumption; these judgments also influence actual consumption (Chandon, Ordabayeva, 2009).

In addition, visual distortions can affect estimates of spaces and distance traveled. Dannhoferová (2012) is of the opinion that the color image conveyed by the visual system does not exactly correspond to reality. It is not only influenced by the quality of vision but also by people's experiences. The perception of colors is different for each person and constantly changes. Colors have a symbolic meaning for people, what associates with a certain cultural environment that is constant and unchanging.

When it comes to flavor, visual components are crucial when consumers consume common foods. Individuals prefer a certain dish not only because of how it tastes or smells, but also due to how it appears (Stillman, 2002). For example, color affects taste perception (Delwiche, 2004), taste intensity (Zampini et al., 2008), and satiety (Raghubir, Krishna, 1999). DuBose et al. (1980) revealed that consumers misinterpreted various fruit tastes because they were improperly colored. Given the importance of color in consumers' taste perception, the integration of favorable and pleasant visual stimuli, such as well-chosen color options, has the potential to enrich consumers' perception of food and help to have a better product experience, complete with the implementation of multisensory essentials (Aydınoğlu, Sayın, 2016).

Pajonk and Plevová (2015) believe that light serves in the store to facilitate orientation, thanks to sufficient clarity and contrast. It should also contribute to the creation of a pleasant atmosphere that will have a positive effect on the psyche of customers. Its task is to draw attention to the product and increase its attractiveness.

Palfiová (2011) claims that lighting in the store can be divided into basic and accent lighting. The task of basic lighting is to achieve the necessary level of light in the space with an emphasis on basic hygiene and safety criteria. Accent lighting is focused on specific requirements of the store, also the type and character of a displayed product. Emphasis is placed on the lighting angle, intensity, and color shade of the light. The visual marketing strategy focuses on the importance of sensory stimuli such as color, light, theme, graphics, but also spatial arrangement. Together, they participate in the creation and evaluation of the identity of that brand (Randhir et al., 2016).

2.2.2 Audio marketing

According to Hultén, Broweus, and Dijk (2009), the auditory sense is constantly active and cannot be turned off. People live in symbiosis with sounds and determine dimensions of life through them. We are able to keep certain sounds in our memory for a longer time and then recall it in connection with memories linked to their initial hearing.

Audio marketing is also an integral part of our life. As the name implies, this type of marketing uses hearing in its work. Music is a part of us. It evokes memories and emotions and creates atmosphere and mood. Shopping spaces with music evoke more positive emotions in customers than spaces without it.

Despite the fact that hearing is one of the senses people use all the time in the marketing sphere, it is not so much preferred. Through hearing, we perceive 12 % consciously and 50 % unconsciously, which means we receive sounds uncontrolled. Music supports the identity of the given business company. Oliver Dauvers conducted research between 1993 and 1994 in which he discovered that the music played in stores hady a strong influence while shopping. He discovered that popular music, on the other hand, has an impact on how much we spend in a particular store and that classical music has a significantly bigger influence on spending than other music genres (Boček et al., 2009).

A large part of marketing communication is auditory – radio and television advertising messages and songs; ambient music is too heard in business areas, restaurants, hotels and airplanes; there exist characteristic sounds from products, such as the sound for the Intel Pentium chip that one hears every single time when the computer is turning on, or the sounds of mobile phones (Krishna, 2012). Marketers use sound to enhance the power of the point-of-sale experience. From energetic music in teen shops to the relaxing sounds of running water in luxury spas. The sound is fundamental and significant part of experiential shopping (Krishna, 2011).

Sounds have various proven effects on consumer mood, perception, and behavior (Yorkston, 2010). Krishna (2013) defines the relationship of a brand with a particular sound as the sound branding in which slogans, signature tunes, and sounds made by a product are connected with brands. Established associations with certain sounds support brand recognition.

Another common use of sound is in stores as the ambient music. In the retail context, ambient music influences product selection (Areni, Kim, 1993), spent time and pace of shopping (Yalch, Spangenberg, 2000), sales (Mattila, Wirtz, 2001), perception of shopping time (Chebat et al., 1993) and trade perception (Hui et al., 1997).

Areni and Kim (1993) show that playing classical music instead of popular music in a wine cellar increases the purchase of expensive wines. North et al. (1999) display that playing French music in supermarkets positively affects the choice of French wines while playing German music increases the choice of German wines. According to Bitner (1992), sounds affect the brand experience through triggering customer emotions and moods. As a result, most stores play music that they think is appropriate for their product selection and company image. Music influences the purchase decisions of consumers who are constantly exposed to it (even if they are unaware of it). Traders recognize the value of music and utilize it on a regular basis to impact perception and the mood of customers, improve the image of their establishments, and maybe raise sales volume.

However, consumers also gain from the presence of music in the shopping or consuming area because it typically enhances and even improves their overall consumption experience due to its beneficial effects on mood (Chebat et al., 1993).

In-store music also affects the pace of shopping – gentler music causes slower shopping and leads to more purchases because consumers move at a slower pace (Milliman, 1982). When consumers like the background music, they feel that they spent less time shopping compared to the actual amount of real time spent in the store; if they don't like it, despite the short amount of time, they claim to have been there much longer (Yalch, Spangenberg, 2000).

Kovanda (2013) defends this by saying that fast music increases the number of beats per minute, which can excite the human organism. This arousal can be explained as an acceleration of the so-called internal mental clock compared to how the passage of objective time is perceived. The choice of background volume is also important, as is the placement and intensity of the music. The music should be played more quietly in the fitting rooms than on the sales floor. In a store, loud music can create a pleasant atmosphere and encourage customers to buy, but it can be inappropriate in fitting rooms (Sikela, 2014).

Music or congruent sound within the flavor might enhance the experience. North (2012) illustrates the influence of music on customer perception of wine taste: while tasting is supported with music that corresponds to the surrounding environment (the wine's place of origin), the taste experience is enhanced. Zampini and Spence (2004) reported that when the sound of biting into potato chips is louder, the chips taste much fresher.

Boček, Krofiánová et al. (2009) argues that music is an emotional trigger. Classical slow music creates a luxurious atmosphere. Musical style can influence which product a customer chooses. Music in advertising influences ad persuasion by influencing mood, as well as engagement (MacInnis, Park, 1991). Music, like the sound of brand names, may contain meaning – both embodied (e.g., a quicker pace might elicit more positive sensations; Stout, Leckenby, 1988) and referential (a nursery rhyme takes us back to childhood; Zhu, Meyers-Levy, 2005). Language may have its own connections, just as the sound of a brand name might lead to a specific image of a product.

According to Krishna and Ahluwalia (2008), certain generalizable language connections exist in bilingual societies that use English as a second language. The usage of English in commercials implies a societal stereotype – a sign of progress, sophistication, modernity and cosmopolitanism (Bhatia, 2000). According to Krishna and Ahluwalia (2008), the identical advertising phrase in English and Hindi has distinct associations. Because the lexical meaning of terms is the same, the explanation for these correlations was not studied. One probable explanation is the subject's connections with the language's sound.

2.2.3 Aroma marketing

The fragrance has been working as a marketing tool since time immemorial, although initially, it was a by-product of other activities, such as cooking or baking. It was only over time that it began to be used purposefully to evoke emotions in a specific person. A person who is in a state of pleasant mood and attunement is of course more impressionable (Štibinger, 2010).

Marketers must astonish consumers and capture their interest in the offered good or service if they want to boost sales. Aroma marketing, often known as fragrance marketing, is one of the most recent strategies for boosting sales. Marketers employ this strategy to arouse clients' emotions through the sense of smell. Aromamarketing is focused on the targeted use of scents for marketing purposes. The sense of smell is very easily influenced, and this form does not bother the customer in any way. Specific scents can stimulate the senses and create new emotions in customers. Through the effects of scents on the premises, merchants can purposefully change the behavior of customers and improve their overall customer experience.

Krishna (2011) believes that the uniqueness of smell compared to other senses lies in its direct connection with memory. This physical, as well as neural proximity of the systems, is the primary reason that information acquired through smell can be retained in memory much longer than information obtained through other senses. According to Lindström (2010), scent is one of the most significant and sensitive senses. He believes that scent is responsible for up to 75 % of emotions. The specific memories associated with a scent determine whether it evokes favorable or bad feelings. Because memories are founded on prior experience, a smell may be pleasant to one individual but not to another.

The scent is directly related to memories and emotions. An aroma might elicit memories and feelings that individuals had when they were exposed to the exact scent in the past. For example, when individuals smell freshly cooked cookies, they frequently recall memories of childhood of mothers preparing cookies. Exposure to the same odor in a new place might elicit the same emotions if they were joyful and safe at the time (Cahill et al., 1995). As a result, many firms include aromas in their products to create an emotional link betwenn memory and smell (Krishna, 2013).

In addition, Krishna et al. (2010) report that customers remember more of the attributes of an unscented product to a scented product compared. Once customers form an association between brand and a scent, memories of the brand will be brought to mind each time they are revealed to the same scent.

The smell of food and drinks is associated with consumer satisfaction and well-being. Food smell is a significant aspect in determining its freshness. People, for example, smell milk before consuming it to see if it has expired. The sense of scent is also very significant in food perception. People who cannot smell have difficulty distinguishing various meals and drinks based only on their taste (Herz, 2007). To put it another way, olfactory stimulation is required to recognize and appreciate the flavor of food (Wysocki, Pelchat, 1993).

Boček, Jesenský, and Krofiánová (2009) claim that the presence of a scent that matches the theme and products in the store has a positive effect on the evaluation of the place itself, but also on products vended there. Some studies confirm that fragrance diffusion can affect the time spent in the store. Vesecký (2015) states that, in principle, the use of aroma marketing can be divided into two basic categories. The first one represents the product use of fragrance, which can directly influence the customer's purchase decision.

Researchers have investigated how olfactory system (smell) influences product or store appraisal and time spent at the store. Pleasant fragrances, according to research, can boost product and shop evaluations and encourage variety-seeking behavior (Bosmans, 2006). (Mitchell et al., 1995). According to Bosmans (2006), ambient fragrance might cause semantic linkage with emotion-based memories (for example, roses and newborns) and boost product rating. When ratings were low, product ratings increased with an ambient scent. Merchants scent spaces or stores with pleasant and specific scents as part of complex marketing communication, thanks to which they support the senses of customers and thereby guarantee that the customer will more easily remember how he felt in this space.

2.2.4 Haptic marketing

According to Grunwald (2008), touch is an integral part of the healthy development of every person. Touch can be considered the core of perception and the basis of communication with the surrounding world. It is the most intimate sense that accompanies a person throughout his life. Hultén, Broweus, and Dijk (2009) claim that touch works through tactile receptors in the skin. With any touch, these receptors send signals to the cerebral cortex. It allows you to feel and recognize heat, cold, roughness, smoothness, pain, or other sensations.

Haptic marketing uses knowledge from psychology. Each product packaging evokes certain emotions in the customer. For example, some prefer plastic bottles, others glass bottles. Some prefer fabric interiors of cars, others leather car interiors (Jesenský et al., 2018). With the help of touch, the customer can receive this one stimulus and feel what he comes into contact with. It is directly focused only on the given product.

Peck and Wiggins (2006) highlight a difference between instrumental and self-serving the need for touch. Some people are more and less affected by touch's influence, but the main difference between people lies in their own preferences, particularly when it comes to getting and using information that they directly experience through touch.

Some people like to evaluate things by physical contact, and they are irritated if they are unable to handle the object when buying. This divides a described desire for touch into 2 components: instrumental and self-serving. Touch offers a chance for those with a greater instrumental demand to get important information about the product that they cannot obtain in other methods, such as reading package leaflets or visual examination. People with a strong self-serving need, on the other hand, tend to touch items just because it is pleasant for them and provides some amount of pleasure. These individuals are more concerned with sensory experience of touch than with the meaning it brings.

Some people like to evaluate things by physical contact, and they are irritated if they are unable to handle the object when buying. This divides a described desire for touch into 2 components: instrumental and self-serving. Touch offers a chance for those with a greater instrumental demand to get important information about the product that they cannot obtain in other methods, such as reading package leaflets or visual examination. People with a strong self-serving need, on the other hand, tend to touch items just because it is pleasant for them and provides some amount of pleasure. These individuals are more concerned with sensory experience of touch than with the meaning it brings (Lederman, Klatzky, 2009).

The degree of touch that customers exhibit when shopping varies (Peck, Childers, 2003). While some customers use their hands to select things off the shelves, others extensively investigate them with hands before making a purchase choice. The structure of a shirt, for example, is more important when making a purchasing choice for customers who have a larger urge to touch items. Some customers spend enormous sums for silk shirts just because they enjoy the delicate texture (Aydınoğlu, Sayın, 2016).

Haptic feelings are not isolated only to hands. People have haptic receptors on skin, all over bodies, and even inside the lips (Krishna, 2013). As a result, the impression of temperature is considered a part of the haptic experience.

The temperature in the store should be ideal so customers feel comfy and spend more time there. Furthermore, haptic receptors in the tongue influence flavor perception. McDaniel (1977) illustrates that customers perceive potato chips in more difficult-to-open packages taste better. Consumers believe that the harder-to-open bags have a superior seal and keep the chips fresher. Krishna and Morrin (2008) report that water served in a glass cup is perceived as tastier compared to when served in a plastic cup.

This type of marketing is mainly used in in-store communication when the customer has the opportunity to examine the properties, overall design, comfort, and others by touch (Krishna, 2010). Marketers base their concepts on haptic communication. Some use minimalist style, designer products, i.e., clean lines characterized by smooth materials, e.g., glass, wood, or metal, and the distribution of these products in the store (Jesenský et al., 2018). While the earlier cases are about touching items, touching humans can also have surprising results. It has been demonstrated that when a waitress directly touches a customer, her tip improves, even if service is not seen as excellent (Crusco, Wetzel, 1984).

The physiological association between generosity and touch was investigated by evolutionary biologists (Morhenn et al., 2008). They wanted to see if oxytocin levels increased after being touched. Oxytocin levels have been demonstrated to increase kindness toward strangers and are also present during labor contractions and orgasms. They discovered that touching raised oxytocin levels when it was followed by an intended gesture of trust.

In addition to people touching objects and people touching others, products touching each other may influence how customers react to those products. Products collide on store shelves, in our shopping carts, and in our home cabinets. Does it matter what touches what? So, if any of the goods make you sick. While all of the above touch effects had beneficial outcomes, we believe that touch might also have negative outcomes. Quite a few of the best-selling items in supermarkets are mildly disgusting, among them garbage bags, cat litter, cigarettes, sanitary napkins, and diapers (Morales, Fitzsimons, 2007). If disgusting objects touch non-disgusting objects, such as placing potato chips next to tampons in your shopping cart or on a shelf, the appeal of the potato chips is reduced. But if you have them near but not touching them, they don't. According to the law of contagion, when a source object contacts a target object, the source continues to impact the target even after it stops touching it (Rozin, Nemeroff, 1990). This rule is related to sympathetic magic laws in that the source magically transmits some of its attributes to the recipient via contact (Nemeroff, Rozin, 1994). Physical contact between the target object and the unpleasant source item appears to evoke feelings of distaste for the infected things.

The rules of contagion apply not just between items, but also betweenn individuals and goods. Argo, Dahl, and Morales (2006) discovered that if another customer had already handled a product, participants loved it less and were less likely to purchase it. They asked research participants to look for and try on a certain T-shirt. The study was organized so that one-third of the participants found the shirt hanging on the shopping rack as normal, another third found it on the return hook in the change room, and the final third found it in the dressing room. It indicates that contamination should have grown from the shopping rack to the return rack to the dressing room as physical contact with the contaminate grew. Product ratings and purchase intents were greatest for the t-shirt on the shopping rack and lowest for the t-shirt in the changeroom, despite the fact that all of the t-shirts were in perfect condition and had never been worn by anyone else. The mere mention of contamination influenced people's assessments.

According to Boek et al. (2009), holding and feeling the product during the purchasing process is a significant action. The ability to touch the product or store brings the customer closer.

2.2.5 Taste marketing

The goal of marketing with an emphasis on taste is to increase the quality of the product perceived by the consumer and to create new sources of inspiration that will affect the imagination and taste experiences of the consumer. We find the use of taste marketing mainly in the food industry. Merchants use it in connection with tastings, which they carry out directly at the point of sale and with the help of which they try to evoke the customer's taste for the given product and subsequently its purchase. It is important not to create a feeling of satisfaction during tastings, e.g., when tasting sweets, because the customer will no longer buy this product. Taste marketing is primarily concerned with food goods and their enhancement, whether it is refining their inherent scent or developing new flavor harmonies. It is influential to experiment with extremely subtle subtleties and unusual flavor and food composition combinations. The French festival, for example, provided a menu with unique and inventive taste combinations of ice cream, such as mint with licorice, apricot with ginger, rose with lychee, and so on (Boček et al., 2009).

Taste, as one of the sensory methods, reflects much more than just the flavor itself, according to Hultén (2011). It is a symbiotic relationship of all five senses. Taste is a concept that combines how a thing smells, looks, feels, and sounds. As a result of the aforementioned interplay and synergy between multiple senses, taste is related with the consumer's multisensory perception. Boček et al. (2009) note fizzy candies that pop in the mouth as an example. These candies stimulate the consumer's perceptions and feelings, which induce a feeling of lightness. Here you can see the impact of tactile marketing.

Taste is the most vulnerable to environmental effects. As previously said, the appearance of the food, its scent, the sound of eating or the ambient music in the background, as well as the texture of the meal, all influence taste perception. When people are unable to see or smell the food, only tasting is usually insufficient to recognize it (Aydnolu, Sayn, 2016). According to Herz (2007), without the smell and the appearance of meals, people cannot tell the difference between an apple and a potato. Brands provide consumers with more satisfying taste experiences by giving multisensory signals and information about beverages and foods (Aydnolu, Sayn, 2016).

This marketing form can be used for cosmetic products such as lip balms or glosses. Thanks to the aroma and fruity taste, it can affect several senses, and at the same time, it creates a pleasant atmosphere. Given the number of commercials that consumers see on a daily basis for the thousands of items on the market, it appears that subconscious triggers, such as those that appeal to fundamental sensations, may be a more successful strategy to attract consumers. These sensory stimuli can also lead to non-consumers self-generating (desirable) brand qualities instead of those presented orally by the marketer. Deductive engagement may be more convincing than explicit claims (Sengupta, Gorn, 2002).

Sensory marketing is, in some ways, the application of sensation and perception understanding to the field of marketing – to customer perception, cognition, learning, emotion, preference, assessment (Krishna, 2011).

3 Neuromarketing

Modern marketing theory and practice are attracted to neuromarketing. Jerry Zaltman (2004) is credited with the development of neuromarketing in the 1990s. He suggested that brain imaging technologies might be used in marketing throughout these years.

The first neuromarketing division was established by the Atlanta company Bright House in 2001. Neuromarketing is a kind of fusion between the interdisciplinary science of neuroscience (the study of the nervous system) and marketing, which opens up space for progress in understanding how people make decisions and how marketers can influence these decisions (neuroscience serves and adapts to the needs of marketing) (Droulers, 2007).

Neuromarketing is a research methodology based on neuroscience, according to Kozel (2011). The information obtained through neuromarketing can be extremely readily misapplied, particularly by big businesses who modify their marketing strategies to appeal to the brain. It is relatively common, especially globally. In the Slovak Republic, a few neurological organizations work with marketing agencies, but only on a more general level (Šášiková, 2013).

Slovakia is more cautious when it comes to neuromarketing research since it is concerned about the misuse of its findings. In Slovakia, establishing collaboration between marketers and neuroscientists is challenging as well due to a lack of funding, enthusiasm, or uncertainty on how useful it would be to businesses. Most Slovak businesses are unable to pay the high cost of research tools and neuromarketing agency services. Media and research agencies in Slovakia do offer neuromarketing services, but they are mostly an additional service offered by their classic marketing research. Instruments, equipment, and neuromarketing services for the research are expensive and unfeasible for smaller companies (Šášiková, 2013).

In the case of neuromarketing research, its final price cannot be determined in advance, which depends on the individual assignments of clients and the use of specific devices. At this point, it is important to mention technologies used in neuromarketing (Vasiľová, Dražová, 2015):

1. *Functional magnetic resonance imaging* (fMRI from the English functional magnetic resonance imaging), a non-invasive neuroimaging technology, is a research method without directly interfering with the human brain, which allows researchers to isolate neuron systems belonging to individual brain functions. Based on changes in local perfusion (fluid flow through a certain

environment) and oxygen consumption, the so-called BOLD effect detects those parts of the cerebral cortex that participate in the realization of a cognitive or motor task (Figure 3.1).
2. *The method of Positron emission tomography*, but due to implementation and time requirements, it is hardly used.
3. *Eye camera*: a less expensive alternative that tracks the movement of the eyes and their stay on certain parts of the displayed surface.
4. *Emo Scan* can scan the face and reactions to various stimuli via a webcam.

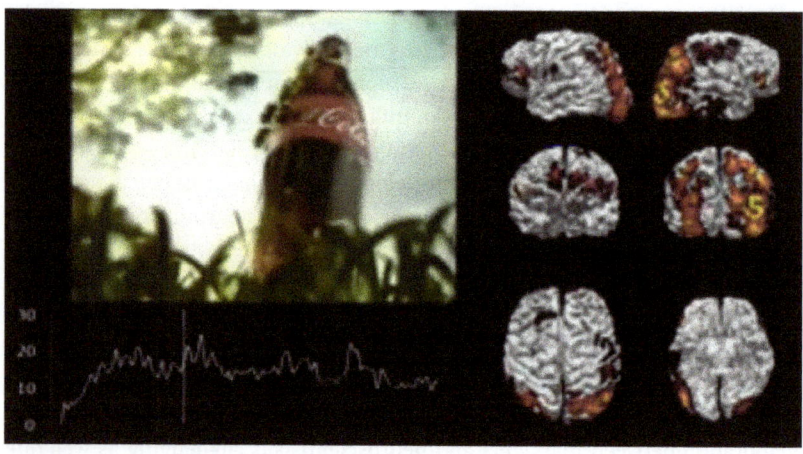

Figure 3.1. Tracking brain activity with fMRI while watching Coca-Cola ad
(*Source:* Das, 2009)

The neuromarketing firm Dicio Marketing 2009 was founded in Slovakia in 2009, and it conducted its first experiments there in 2007. For the Good Angel organization, the initial tests were conducted. For tests in 2009, the agency used 24-channel EEG Brain Master Discovery technology (from the US), which allows for the measurement of brain activity. The agency is the first in Slovakia to use experience and knowledge from the functioning of the brain when interpreting classic qualitative and quantitative research (Švec, 2014).

With the use of neuromarketing research using techniques, methods, EEG, and fMRI instruments, the seller may, if not force, at least convince his clients to think more seriously about purchasing the product. Some authors of neuromarketing monographs believe that neuromarketing has such a profound effect on them that they begin to accept the idea that there is a "buy button" that compels consumers to purchase a product (Samuhelová, Šimková, 2015).

According to the paradigms and expertise of neuroscience, neuromarketing is the study of mental, implicit, and explicit processes, consumer behavior in various marketing scenarios, as well as assessment, decision-making, memorizing, and consumption processes. The importance of neuromarketing is, therefore, in the expansion and accumulation of knowledge of an interdisciplinary nature, related to consciousness and the brain, in their practical use in marketing practice (Samuhelová, Šimková, 2015).

Aydınoğlu and Sayın (2016) state that all examples from academic research demonstrate the importance of sensory cues in product marketing, especially in creating a favorable and enriched customer experience and influencing consumer perception and behavior. Accordingly, marketers and academics are highly motivated to understand these effects through multiple methodological approaches. By analyzing customer behavior or gathering self-evaluative reactions following exposure to relevant sensory stimuli, the majority of research in sensory marketing examines the effects of sensory stimuli. Self-evaluation is crucial when determining the underlying causes of various customer reactions.

Some researchers criticize the reliability of self-report measures and point to their limitations. Schafer (2005) notes: "Neither every Coca-Cola consumer knows what drives him to his favorite drink, nor can he objectively describe the impulse, given the influence of marketing he has already been exposed to." In addition, experts also suggest concerns related to data on consumer self-reports, where they note that "consumers either lie to themselves or tell what they think we want to hear" (Walton, 2004). The ability and willingness of respondents to appropriately report their attitudes or prior behavior is therefore frequently stated to be over-relied upon in self-report methods (Petty, Cacioppo, 1983).

These concerns have led to the deployment of various techniques that attempt to measure the physiological responses accompanying the cognitive, affective, and conative processes that consumers go through. This line of work rests on the claim that most body systems are active during cognitive and emotional activities (Aydınoğlu, Sayın, 2016). From the beginning, electrodermal activity (EDA) was investigated by observing changes in skin conductivity, or the expansion and contraction of the pupils of the eyes.

Morin (2011a, 2011b) points to the lack of traditional research, which is primarily dependent on the will and abilities of researched subjects, and subsequently describes what they feel when they are exposed to advertising, decide to buy a product or service, or when they consume this product. The research participant has to verbalize his answers, which leads to some degree of distorted data within his expressive abilities. A subjective statement about oneself, i.e., self-report, also means that participants can consciously lie, but also they can react as they think is expected of them. On the other hand, with neuroimaging techniques, the reaction of participants to stimuli is investigated directly, even without being processed by cognitive and conscious processes.

Human sense research indicates that senses such as hearing, sight, touch, smell, and feeling can impact preferences, memory, and decision (Krishna, 2011). According to Jang and Namkung (2009), the structural and sensory stimuli of the store improve the consumer experience. Some senses influence memory and cognition, but the scent has the greatest influence on it (Krishna, 2011).

According to neuromarketing research, the brain will process an individual stimulus as a sense, which will be processed cognitively in the brain, and emotions will be processed in the limbic system, which will generate a perception of the item or stimulus. Common sense dictates that the more favorable sensory stimuli provided by the marketer to the consumer, the more positive the customer's view of the brand will be (Riza, Wijayanti, 2018).

In the context of food consumption, physiological measurements focused on cephalic phase responses (CPR). CPRs are evoked by exposure to sensory aspects of food (for example, appearance, taste, and smell) as well as just thinking about eating (Nederkoorn et al., 2000). In this scenario, saliva is the most commonly utilized measurement. Salivation is seen as a beneficial indication of desire for food stimulus that is not under the consumer's conscious control (Pecina, Smith, 2010).

There are numerous ways for monitoring salivary flow, including counting the number of times individuals swallow over time (Nederkoorn et al., 2000), allowing saliva to flow into a test tube, periodic spitting (Jenkins, Dawes, 1964), and whole-mouth suction with a vacuum pump (Herman et al., 1981). Measures of salivation, as well as simple statements of food cues or instructions to imagine food products, have been employed in marketing and consumer behavior to explore the effects of different sensory components of food (Krishna et al., 2014).

Incorporating knowledge from numerous scientific disciplines, including neurology, psychology, sociology, and last but not least, marketing itself, neuromarketing is a modern and relatively new discipline (the concept of its origin dates to 1990 in the USA). It is a marketing technique that uses the application of neuroscience to achieve a more accurate reading of customer behavior. Typical neuromarketing activities include direct examination of the customer's brain and mind, scanning or other technologies for measuring brain activity to observe the customer's reaction to certain elements of the product, including its packaging, price, advertising, and other marketing elements (Fischer et al., 2010).

Because neuromarketing argues that human decision-making (buying) is not as conscious as previously supposed (consumer decisions rely on 80 % unconscious behavior), the phrase homo economicus appears to be obsolete. This is why neuromarketing is sometimes referred to as the science of human decision-making. A limited definition of neuromarketing is a market research method that employs medical gadgets, but a rigorous definition is the incorporation of brain research findings into economic theory and practice. At first glance, the confluence of these two scientific fields, neurology and marketing, may appear unusual. Neuromarketing is a highly intriguing subject in which medicine joins the art of marketing to investigate the continuous subconscious processes of the human brain (Roth, 2013). So it's about how to sell products and services to people so that they want them more and buy them sooner. We often think we know why we act this way or another, but in reality, it's just stories we unconsciously make up to explain our actions (Lorincz, 2009).

The subject of the investigation is the customer's purchasing behavior, i.e., the purchase decision process. It examines the brain, which ultimately influences decision-making when purchasing products. This customer decision can be rational or irrational depending on the influence of external factors (Šášiková, 2013).

According to Müller (2019), neuromarketing defines four key human factors:

1. Eye perception – What do we perceive, how perceive, and why?
2. Knowledge – What do we use in our decision-making?
3. Appeal – What do we find attractive and what don't?
4. Decisions – What factors influence the final decision?

The first and basic characteristic of neuromarketing is the use of techniques mapping neural and physiological activity. The main methods used in neuromarketing are Functional magnetic resonance imaging (fMRI), Electroencephalography (EEG), and Magnetoencephalography (MEG). Neuroimaging techniques are classically used in neurology, the medical field that studies diseases of the nervous system. The inability to directly examine customer behavior and its correlates, such as the impact of advertising, the choice to purchase, or the experience of making this purchase, has led to the desire to apply these techniques in marketing research. Investigating the neural background in neuromarketing, for example, which area of the brain is activated during the presentation of a particular object, gives a more valid answer to the questions that are investigated in the research (Dapkevicius, Melnikas, 2009).

The aforementioned methods present possibilities for analyzing consumer behavior, but it's important to consider their limitations and the accuracy of the data interpretation. All research using neuroimaging techniques requires the participation of an experienced neuroscientist. With the use of neuroimaging techniques, it is also necessary to take into account the high costs of neuromarketing research. According to Kotler (2013), projects can cost up to $100,000. The laboratory environment, where the majority of the tests are conducted, is also unique compared to traditional research. The generalizability of the inferences made from observations made under natural circumstances is under doubt. The lower number of participants in the research also results from the high costs and the need for a demanding examination of each respondent. In most investigations that used, for example, functional magnetic resonance, the number of participants varied between 20 and 60 respondents. Solnais et al. (2013) state that the average number of respondents in neuromarketing studies is 24. Investigating physical activity, which the respondent is not aware of, often raises the question of the ethics of neuromarketing research. This concern raises uncertainty regarding the misuse of the obtained data.

Bercea (2013) believes that neuromarketing belongs to quantitative research precisely because it is based on the hypotheses it tries to test. However, it also carries elements of qualitative research, especially in that it respects the heterogeneity of a smaller research sample and tries to comprehensively explain the results. Focus is placed on sensory investigation, recognition, emotional reactions to marketing stimuli, preferences, driving forces, expectations, and future behavior in neuromarketing. The most well-known studies examined the influence of the brand on the actual taste experience (Kenning, Plassmann, 2005); the analysis of purchase decisions (Braeutigam et al., 2001); price perception, the purchasing process (Knutson, Greer, 2008).

Neuromarketing examines the sensorimotor, cognitive, and affective reactions of customers to marketing stimuli to find out why and how consumers make decisions (Kozel et al., 2011; Oláh, Fogašová, 2013). From the given definition, we can derive the basic idea of neuromarketing – to find out what emotions people experience when they watch TV, read a magazine, in short, when they are exposed to communication. We know very well what they say or what they do with explicit research methods and techniques that are now routinely known. The implicit approach represents neuromarketing techniques, which can be more advantageous and interesting in certain cases than quantitative or qualitative research because it also provides insight into the customer's subconscious, which frames the decision-making process.

Lindström (2009) thinks that neuromarketing is a tool by which it is possible to find out what the customer thinks about the products or specific brands of the given products. Through neuromarketing, we can also detect unfair business practices of traders. Neuromarketing tries to explain why and how what consumers tell us in research differs from what they do. In contrast to the explicit approach, the implicit approach also shows advantages in the form of not obtaining information through a system of questions and answers, thus minimizing possible mutual misunderstanding between the researcher and the respondent.

The use of neuromarketing pursues a certain sales goal, which is then used by companies to determine what products and brands to produce using this research. Neuromarketing also significantly affects advertising.

Typical marketing research has several differences from neuromarketing research. Neuromarketing is more demanding concerning human research and concerning the use of devices. While typical marketing is largely based on a cross-section of customers, through unverifiable methods (target groups, surveys, customer records, etc.), neuromarketing focuses on individual marketing test subjects, usually no more than a few dozen or more, over a longer period (Majba, 2018).

Neuromarketing is the process of examining the brains of consumers to discover their reactions to specific advertisements and products before developing new advertising campaigns and brands. In practice, the direction of eye gaze is especially important in advertising. Ads that feature people are much more effective than ads that don't feature them. In particular, images and videos that contain children tend to attract longer and more intense attention from potential customers. Advertisers have long tried to boost sales for children's products by using adorable baby faces — but with the help of new neuromarketing discoveries, they've found that alone isn't enough. Researchers have found that when a child is facing you, viewers will focus more on the child's face at the expense of the ad's content. If the child directs his look to the product or text, then the viewer focuses on the advertising content (Majba, 2018). Color is also important as it can affect how potential customers feel. Numerous emotions can be evoked by colors, and studies repeatedly link particular shades to particular emotions.

Because it combines the principles of psychology, neurology, economics, and marketing, neuromarketing is a ground-breaking concept in the field of marketing research. The concept behind neuromarketing is that it depends on sensory stimuli, particularly visual cues for the perception of names, trademarks, and logos, which creates a close connection with the brand. Companies rely on this idea of visual stimulation to effectively sell their products. As we mentioned in the previous chapter, the sound, colors, atmosphere, touch, smell, music, and architecture of some branded stores have a pleasant effect on the customer, and consumers not only connect with the brand but are forced to shop in these stores and recommend them to friends and family. This experience is also used by hotels and restaurants that study their target consumers and try to meet their specific needs using the results of neuromarketing (Elangovan, Padma, 2017).

The significant rise of neuromarketing techniques, which have provided new strategic possibilities, allow marketers to probe the brains of consumers to gain valuable insights into the subconscious processes that explain why an advertising message ultimately succeeds or fails. Marketers eliminate the biggest problem facing conventional advertising research, which is the belief that people have both the motivation and the ability to express how a particular advertisement excites them (Morin, 2011a, 2011b).

Wilson et al. (2008) compare stages of marketing research in the traditional research model and the neuromarketing research model:

1. *Screening phase*: a sample of potential consumers is exposed to marketing stimuli, while in the second model of purchasing behavior (Figure 3.3) the brain activity of the examined sample is observed using fMRI technology, while in the traditional model (Figure 3.2) marketers use classic in-depth group interviews. In both cases, the output from this phase is information that enables adaptation or targeting activities aimed at motivating the consumer to purchase.
2. *Intervention phase*: occurs at the moment when the consumer is affected by the communication activity, his cognitive and affective processes are activated and attitudes and intentions towards the purchase are formed. While in the traditional model, this phase represents a black box in which the consumer's consciousness is inaccessible to the researcher, the second model, thanks to the use of neuroscience, provides information about reactions to sensory stimuli, as well as memories obtained by exposure to stimuli in the past.
3. *The last phase*: the decision to buy or not buy the product, includes the consequences of these decisions, both positive and negative, on society as well as on the individual.

Neuromarketing 53

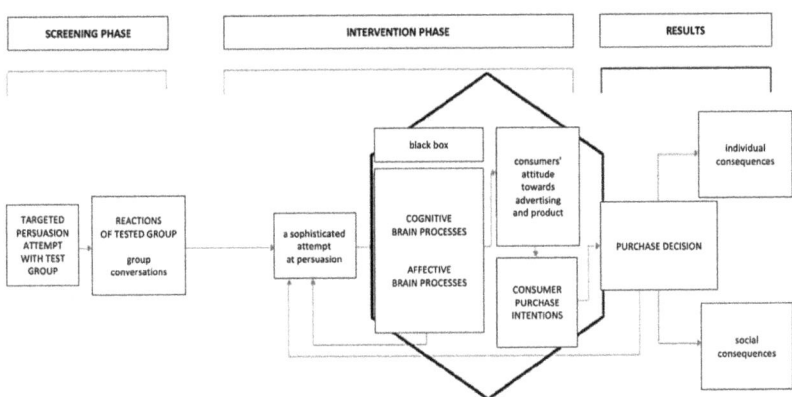

Figure 3.2. Traditional model of shopping behavior
(*Source:* Wilson et al., 2008)

Figure 3.3 shows the use of neuromarketing methods in consumer research

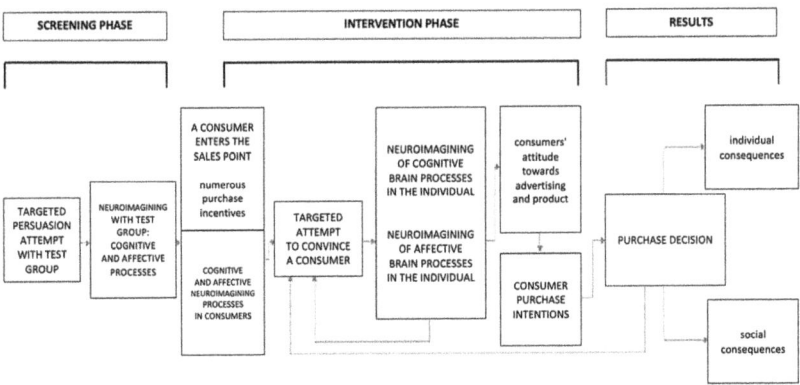

Figure 3.3. Model of shopping behavior with the use of neuromarketing
(*Source:* Wilson et al., 2008)

Neuromarketing applies neuropsychology to marketing research. It examines the sensorimotor, cognitive, and affective reactions of customers to marketing stimuli. It employs technologies like electroencephalography (EEG) and steady-state topography (SST) to measure activity in particular regional brain response spectra, functional magnetic resonance imaging (fMRI) to measure changes in activity in certain brain areas, functional magnetic resonance imaging (fMRI) to measure changes in activity in specific areas of the brain, sensors to monitor changes in your physiological state (also known as biometrics), such as heart rate, breathing rate, and galvanic skin response, facial coding to classify the physical manifestation of emotion, or eye tracking to identify focus (Majba, 2018). A closer description of neuromarketing techniques is given in the next subsection.

3.1 Neuroscience

Experts in the field of neuromarketing tried to find out why some research results do not correspond to reality. They found that new methods and strategies producing more accurate scientific data were lacking. The reason quantitative and qualitative marketing research is not always objective is that the people interviewed may not be telling the truth and may not even know it by themselves. Respondents mostly make decisions irrationally, without thinking, based on their emotions and feelings. The respondent can be affected by various factors that distort his answers. They are, for example, emotions. It would be the most useful to capture these influencing factors on paper, but this is not possible in any normal and controlled conversation. Therefore, they must be captured in the brain as soon as they arise. Thanks to this, a new scientific field was created – neuromarketing (Lindström, 2009).

In recent years, the development of neuroscience has significantly changed the understanding of the brain and its functioning thanks to advances in the field of molecular biology, electrophysiology, and the sophistication of computers. Advances have enabled neuroscientists to study the nervous system in all its aspects. This field has greatly contributed to a better understanding of human behavior (Zurawicki, 2010).

We define neuroscience as a scientific discipline that deals with the study of the nervous system due to its development, structure, and natural principles of functioning. Neuroscience experts base their research on the influence of brain activities on human behavior from this knowledge (Morris, 2003).

Neuroscience is a fusion of various disciplines, bringing together molecular biology, neuropsychology, anatomy, developmental biology, cell biology, behavioral psychology, neurology, cognitive neuropsychology, and cognitive science into one. This relatively new field of research has contributed significantly to a better understanding of human behavior in recent years. It also provides information on consumer behavior (Zurawicki, 2010).

For marketing and marketing research, neuroscience is very important. Across a wide range of products and brands, neuroscience is increasingly important to consumers and manufacturers. Neuroscience helps to reveal the true wishes of interviewees using devices that measure brain activity (Plessis, 2011).

The body's primary mechanism for control, regulation, and communication is the nervous system. The brain, spinal cord, nerves, and ganglia make up the majority of it. These, in turn, are composed of several cell types, such as connective tissue, blood, and nerves. Through its receptors, the nervous system keeps people connected to their internal and external environments. Together with endocrine hormone activity, the nervous system regulates and maintains the balance of the body and every part of our life.

According to Zurawicky (2010), the various activities of the nervous system can be grouped as three general interconnected functions:

- sensory,
- integrative,
- movement.

The nervous system is the main control and inseparable system of the organism. Its main function is a fast and accurate transmission of information from receptors, their central processing, and the transmission of new signals to effectors (Hošková, 2012).

The nervous system also acts as the center of all mental activities, such as thinking, learning, and memory. From an anatomical and functional point of view, according to Zurawický (2010), the nervous system has the following two main components:

1. *The central nervous system*, composed of the brain and spinal cord – much better for studying consumer behavior. The brain acts as an integrator of incoming stimuli and as a command center. The spinal cord extends the central nervous system from the brain and is enclosed and protected by the bony column. The main function of the spinal cord is the transmission of nerve inputs between the periphery and the brain.
2. *Peripheral nervous system composed of nerves* – these systems are relatively primitive and cannot be regulated at the peripheral level. They can be controlled at a central level, e.g., when we rationally choose not to pay attention to a certain stimulus or when we rationally choose to ignore a situation that evokes fear.

The human brain is the most complex structure known. The systematic study of this organ is a mystery in itself. It is sufficient to state that the brain contains up to one billion neurons (or nerve cells) interconnected in much larger interconnections to emphasize the complexity of the brain's structure. Uncovering the anatomy of the brain and its neurofunctional composition provides the basis for a better understanding of our daily functioning, creative processes, or artistic expression. The brain is made up of many areas responsible for different tasks. The field of functional neuroanatomy is focused on linking function with brain structure. However, it is important to understand brain activities as a mutual connection of individual parts. No brain region works alone (Zurawicki, 2010).

3.2 Techniques in neuromarketing

Majba (2018) lists three types of techniques that map human neural and physiological activity:

- measuring brain metabolic activity: functional magnetic resonance imaging,
- measuring the electrical activity of the brain: electroencephalography,
- not measuring brain activity: eye camera and biometrics.

Currently, there are several techniques used for functional mapping that use different views. These are mainly the following techniques:

- Functional magnetic resonance imaging (fMRI),
- Electroencephalography (EEG),
- Magnetoencephalography (MEG),
- Positron emission tomography (PET) and so on.

These techniques differ from one another mainly in how they manage spatial and temporal resolution, time and economic constraints, and potential contraindications of the tested individuals. In addition to functional mapping, neuromarketing employs strategies that attempt to reveal latent purposes for tracking eye movements (eye-tracking) (Tyrlíková, a kol., 2012).

3.2.1 Functional Magnetic Resonance (fMRI)

It is an imaging technique that has been used in medicine since the 1970s. By using fMRI, experts obtain reliable and valid measurements of cognitive and affective responses (Wang, Elhag, 2008). This technique is based on the fact that brain activity is related to brain function. Therefore, we can localize the neural activity that accompanies consumer decision-making during the purchasing process. Due to its properties, magnetic resonance is suitable not only for examining the brain but also for examining the heart, blood vessels, and abdominal and pelvic organs (Válek, Žižka, 1996).

Functional magnetic resonance is mainly used in neuromarketing for testing new products, and campaigns, testing and developing advertising, identifying key moments in advertising, and testing packaging and prices. It is also used to identify customer needs and for sensory testing (Bercea, 2011). The technique is used in up to 70 % of research dealing with the neuropsychology of consumer behavior (Kable, 2011).

3.2.2 Electroencephalography (EEG)

It is the second most used technique in neuromarketing (Bercea, 2011). Davidson's study from 1979 is considered the first psychological study using data from EEG measurements (Vysekalová, 2011). It presents a non-invasive technique that senses the electrical activity of the brain using electrodes. These are placed on the surface of the head and sense changes in bioelectrical potentials. As part of neuromarketing, the EEG can be used as a portable device and used to measure brain activity in conditions other than the laboratory, for example when shopping in a store. Using the ability of fast time resolution, EEG is used to analyze brain activity while watching television advertising (Vysekalová, 2011). The advantages of EEG include easier handling compared to fMRI, the possibility of device portability, and fast temporal resolution. Compared to other devices, it is a cheaper device (Ariely, Berns, 2010).

3.2.3 Magnetoencephalography (MEG)

This technique measures the magnetic field that realizes the electric current during the passage of ions through the cell membrane on the dendritic and axonal processes of neurons. However, the magnetic field is very weak, but it can still be captured. The device that detects the magnetic field on the surface of the head is called a magnetometer. The advantage of this technique is very good time resolution (Kulišťák, 2003).

3.2.4 Computed Tomography (CT)

The essence of computed tomography is based on the measurement of absorption values of X-ray radiation that passes through the human body. The detector detects an electrical signal analyzed by a computer (Kulišťák 2003). Tomography originates from the Latin word tomeo, which means to cut. In tomography, images of sections of individual layers of a body part are collected. The advantage of CT is lower costs than fMRI examination (Nevšímalová, Růžička, Tichý, 2002).

3.2.5 Positron Emission Tomography (PET)

It is a device that captures a physiological image of metabolism by recording the radiation that is induced by a radioactive substance that was administered to a person for measurement (Válek, 1998).

3.2.6 Near-Infrared Spectroscopy (NIRS)

Spectroscopy is a device that works based on a wavelength similar to infrared radiation. There are two types of NIRS. The first type is EROS (event-related optical signal), which measures the change in intensity of the reflected signal upon stimulation of a certain stimulus. The change is caused by electrical activity in the brain, which changes the ion concentration. It will gradually manifest itself in light scattering, which is recorded. The second is the type used as part of the transformation of blood circulation during brain activity. The advantage of NIRS is that it does not have a negative effect on the body because it does not expose it to radioactive radiation (Koukolík, 2010).

3.2.7 Facial coding

It is a technique where micro-expressions of the face, which cannot be controlled arbitrarily, are monitored and measured using a video camera. As it relates to neuromarketing, it is clear that this technique relates to emotions. Within neuromarketing, the technique is used in testing advertising and movie trailers. It makes it possible to detect emotions by capturing facial expressions without verbally censoring their wearer (Bercea, 2011).

3.2.8 Facial Electromyography (EMG)

EMG uses not only observation to analyze emotions from the facial muscles but also electrodes that are placed on the examined nerve. The electrodes measure the tiny bioelectrical signal caused by the shortening of the muscle fibers. It provides accurate information about the involvement of muscles. Men and women differ in the expression of emotions. Women show higher muscle activity than men on EMG (Dimberg, Lundquist, 1990).

3.2.9 Eye-tracking

Eye-tracking is a technique used for a long time. It has been used in America since the 1960s, and in Europe since the 1980s (Vysekalová, 2012). This technique measures behavior and cognitions without measuring brain activity by examining what a person looks at and for how long. The principle of operation is based on the fact that a person uses sight and eye movements to obtain information from the environment and for their subsequent processing. These movements are engaged at the moment when the image is explored and when the attention is focused on different places. Subsequently, a complex idea of the image or scene is created. The eyes focus on a certain point and, after fixation, make a quick and jerky movement to another place. Eye movements serve to increase the time for which an unchanging image is captured on the retina (Šikl, 2012; Klimeš, 2001).

Zurawicki (2010) states that the first two movements mentioned are the most important for neuromarketing, i.e., fixation and twitching. With this technique, experts try to find out how customers filter information and which elements will be processed earlier and later. So they try to reveal the hierarchy of perceptual stimuli. Eye movements point to unconscious processes, phasic processing of advertising, and measuring competitive rules. Eye-tracking is combined with electroencephalography or functional magnetic resonance imaging in neuromarketing (Tomek, 2011).

Using an eye camera, the Eye tracker examines visual attention and the customer's emotional response using an electroencephalograph (EEG). In addition to researching the customer's purchasing behavior, this method can also be used in the development and creation of the products themselves and their placement in individual markets (Berčík et al., 2014).

3.2.10 Measurement of physiological responses

Physiological reactions can also be measured with a polygraph. It is an electronic device that records the physiological activity of the human body caused by the autonomic nervous system. It is very often used in criminology when it is used as a lie detector. The signals are recorded through sensors attached to a specific point on the human body. A polygraph can be used to assess physiological symptoms like blood pressure, heart rate, or breathing (Bercea, 2011).

Neuromarketing techniques are used to measure deeper responses to various stimuli. For the needs of neuromarketing research, experts can choose from several techniques. They differ in their costs, the difficulty of operation, the demands on the premises, the burden of the examined persons, and the possibilities for the accuracy of displaying neutral activity spatially or temporally. Therefore, it is not possible to determine which of the methods is the best, because each of the techniques is suitable for different uses. Anyway, in practice, these neuroimaging techniques should be combined with traditional methods.

According to Kotler (2013), other approaches should be added to neurological techniques as the foundation for the development of a marketing plan.

3.3 Neuromarketing in the context of the research

Neuromarketing is based on neuroscience and is a new research method. It is dedicated to researching the nervous system and applying neuroscience to the field of marketing. The goal of neuromarketing is to find out how consumer decision-making is influenced, and which part of the brain is activated at the moment of decision-making. For this, he uses, for example, the following medical technologies: magnetic resonance imaging (fMRI), electroencephalography (EEG), etc. (Kozel, 2006).

Neuromarketing, like many newly developing fields, still has a lot of development and research to do. Despite the valuable results it brings, this method is still relatively little used in practice. Not only the already mentioned ethical aspects but also the financial demands of fMRI technology are discouraging. On the other hand, the current interest in human brain research technologies is evident, which only confirms the formation of a new field of marketing research. Neuromarketing is a supplement to classic research techniques such as inquiry or observation (Vasiľová, Dražová, 2015).

Neuromarketing investigates which emotions are important to people when making decisions and uses these findings to make marketing more effective. The findings are applied to product design, improving promotion and advertising, pricing, store design, and improving the overall consumer experience (Sousa, 2018).

Is it possible to observe the sensation in the form of neuromarketing as hope for future marketing research, or is it just a halo effect caused by the vision of perfect knowledge of consumer behavior? Scientists Dan Ariely from the Center for Cognitive Neuroscience at Duke University and Gregory S. Berns from the Department of Psychiatry and Behavioral Sciences at Emory University tried to answer this question.

By studying numerous cases of neuromarketing applications (advertising campaigns for drinks, food, experiential marketing, political campaigns), they obtained empirical knowledge, which they summarized in the following statements (Vasiľová, Dražová, 2015):

1. *Halo effect*: Neuromarketing methods will be a cheaper alternative to traditional marketing research tools and will gradually replace it completely. The same claim was made by Martin Lindström, the author of the publication

Nacupology which has become a current marketing bestseller. However, the cost of fMRI technology cannot be overlooked, and that's why this claim is considered premature and unrealistic.

2. *Hope for future research*: authors state that neuromarketing will soon be able to provide previously undiscovered information about consumer preferences.

It is possible to assume that marketing research will not accomplish without classic research methods, such as in-depth interviews, panels, or observation methods, even in the future. Neuromarketing, on the other hand, still contains many unexplored areas, from which other possibilities of its application may result (Vasiľová, Dražová, 2015).

Wilson a kol. (2008) vymedzuje oblasti budúceho akademického výskumu problematiky neuromarketingu nasledovne:

3.3.1 Creation of trust

Trust in marketing is present in many contexts, whether we are talking about trust in advertising claims, products, nowadays, especially organic products or fair trade, or we understand it as the quality of the relationship between business partners, employees, customers, and the organization. Marketing research is no longer satisfied with the definition of trust as a simple economic calculation. The possibility of using neuroscientific methods in examining the origin and nature of trust in business relationships is increasingly discussed. Researchers ask themselves whether trust is just a reaction to repeated positive stimuli or whether it arises in the same areas of the brain as trust in a partner or friendship. Obtaining information about the origin of trust and its temporal characteristics can in the future lead to the higher efficiency of companies in building the trust and loyalty of customers, employees, or business partners.

3.3.2 Pricing strategy

Understanding the psychology of prices is of key importance in choosing the optimal position for a product. Price research is especially important in cases where information and resources are insufficient and the consumer is forced to weigh the benefits obtained against the costs. The use of neuroscientific methods should enable not only an understanding of how information about prices is processed in the human brain but also answer questions about the psychology of prices, i.e., whether the price of a product is purely rational information, or evokes certain emotions in the consumer.

3.3.3 Negotiation

Consumers often find themselves in situations where they have to negotiate prices and other sales and purchase conditions (buying real estate, cars). When investigating the negotiation process, the method of game theory is used, but recently there has been a growing interest in the application of neuromarketing in the field of research on negotiation behavior. The subject of the investigation is primarily the question of whether emotions prevail among individuals or, on the contrary, rationality when negotiating prices or other conditions of purchase and sale. Neuromarketing could provide information on which parts of the brain are activated when applying risky negotiation tactics to harm the other party.

3.3.4 Ethics

The ethical dilemmas associated with the application of neuroscientific methods in marketing have already been presented in the previous chapter. On the other hand, there is an opinion that neuromarketing could, on the contrary, contribute to the formation of ethical principles in marketing. In addition to searching for the so-called shopping triggers in the consumer's brain, neuromarketing can focus on determining whether certain aspects of advertising and marketing communication result in a negative effect in the form of excessive and irresponsible consumption. Investigating the causes of excessive indebtedness of some consumers, the origin of their compulsive purchases, and the motivations of sales representatives to apply unfair practices when acquiring clients, can also be a subject of neuromarketing.

The proposed areas of research in the context of neuromarketing do not focus exclusively on its commercial application. On the contrary, new focuses of academic research could contribute to a better understanding of the critical issues of contemporary human society. One of the biggest concerns about neuromarketing and consumer behavior is that marketers might discover a buy button that would allow experts to control consumer behavior and compel the consumer to buy. However, these concerns are unfounded (Wilson et al., 2008).

Most research only describes and tries to reveal how the human brain works at the moment of decision in the purchasing process. Experts who support neuromarketing claim that neuroscience can be compared with all other methods that have studied human behavior in the past. This investigation is a method of measuring factors that have not been available until now. Neuromarketing is a more accurate method than manipulating consumer behavior that measures preferences (Wilson, 2008).

The ethical dilemma stems from the fact that the results obtained from research subjects are or can be used to influence their responses (to promote sales, construct promotional communication messages, etc.) without censoring the respondents. Another objection to these studies is that they suspect companies that potentially manipulate consumers to get their reaction or gain their favorable reactions to the organization, regardless of whether the studies carried out have only a purely educational purpose or are intended to thoroughly investigate consumer behavior (Thomas et al., 2017).

Most of the ethical problems can be closed and solved thanks to the Neuromarketing Science and Business Association (NMSBA), which is the organization responsible for formulating the basic principles and rules for conducting research in the field of neuromarketing. The rules must be strictly followed by all neuromarketing agencies within the association, no exceptions are allowed. From the ESOMAR guideline were modified the principles of the NMSBA, which emphasizes the need to observe the ethical principles, not only of neuromarketing itself but of all areas related to it, e.g., medicine and neurology (Thomas et al., 2017).

3.4 Neuromarketing in selected sectors of marketing

In recent years, the prefix neuro has become very popular. This fact supports the emergence of new fields such as neuroeconomics, neuroprogramming, neuroengineering, neuroinformatics, etc. This term has also been appropriated by marketing agencies, as part of its popularity, in an attempt to offer services to customers, which is why they use the word neuromarketing for promotion.

Fisher et al. (2010) in their case study discussed the focus of companies that offer neuromarketing services on the Internet. Of the total number of 16 companies that offered neuromarketing on the Internet, only 5 of them offered the fMRI technique, 9 used EEG, and 12 of them offered other techniques, such as MEG, eye-tracking, skin conductance measurement, electrocardiograph, and the like. One of the companies did not even offer any of these techniques. It offered only common marketing methods such as focus groups, that is, comparing groups and others. However, she mentioned neuromarketing terms during the presentation. Four of these companies had a list of their customers, and only one listed the price list of the services offered. So it is questionable whether real neuromarketing was implemented or if it was a false reporting of services.

When examining scientific articles on the neuropsychology of consumer behavior, it can be argued that at the beginning of the term, the authors attributed unrealistic optimism. Later, articles seemed to be more realistic, where limits and restrictions are also mentioned and discussed more often.

As marketers wish, the buy button can be triggered by a marketing effort, such as advertising, that aims to increase sales or purchases. Advertisers can influence the buy button and create impulse buying behavior. You could say marketers hit the button with desirable products and advertising. However, consumer decision-making is a complex process and behavior over time. Behavior is manifested simultaneously by feelings, emotions, and experiences, including conscious and unconscious processes. Purchasing decisions and behavior are not processed by just one point of the brain, but by many, including the medial frontal cortex, hippocampus, amygdala, etc. Purchase decisions are complex behaviors that take place over time, involve both conscious and unconscious processes, and force trade-offs between the expectation of reward and the pain they have to pay for it. Researchers have found that familiarity with the brand you buy can influence your preferences by controlling brain circuits involved in memory, decision-making, and self-image (Isa et al., 2019).

Consumer decision research focuses on how consumer preferences are formed and how neural activity can be used to predict them. In this area have been conducted many consumer neuroresearches establishing the role of the ventromedial prefrontal cortex in consumer decision-making. Research indicates that the right and left ventromedial prefrontal cortex are responsible for emotional involvement in decision-making (Bechara et al., 2000). An emotional factor is important when making a decision. If consumers experience positive emotional involvement, it is more likely to improve purchasing behavior. One example is the positive emotions evoked by music. Ju and Ahn (2016) reported that music can induce emotional responses such as pleasure and excitement and is significantly related to impulse buying. Although it cannot help marketers to press the buy button in consumers' brains, we can learn from the research that many factors contribute to increasing consumers' purchase intention under different circumstances (Isa et al., 2019).

Products that represent higher status in terms of wealth and social status can influence the brain's reward system. Raab et al. (2011) found that the local brain activation involved in purchasing decisions is different between compulsive and non-compulsive consumers. Non-compulsive consumers showed significantly lower activation, suggesting that compulsive buying behavior may result from a positive relationship of the brain's reward system in response to marketing stimuli.

Hulten (2017) states that a perceived positive brand experience can improve purchasing behavior. A positive brand experience can refer to the pleasure perceived during that experience. Research shows that pleasure and excitement can influence purchase intention. When we feel that a product experience satisfies our needs, we tend to feel satisfied and that's where the brain's reward system comes into play.

According to the acceptance-avoidance model (Davidson, 2004), pleasantness in advertising may be one of the factors that stimulate consumers' motivation to accept products, with greater activation of the brain in the left hemisphere.

Research conducted by Vecchiato et al. (2011) points to differential brain activation related to levels of perceived pleasantness concerning advertising. Pleasantness expresses the degree to which individuals like advertising. Higher pleasantness shows higher neural activation in the left hemisphere, while lower pleasantness shows more brain activation in the right hemisphere. By understanding how neural activities represent emotional responses, marketers can design their advertising and products using these approaches and thus motivate consumers to acquire these products (Isa et al., 2019).

Although neuromarketing cannot help marketers push the buy button in consumers' brains, it can influence consumers' purchase intent. As mentioned above, many factors can influence consumer decision-making and purchasing behavior. Thus, sensory marketing, which focuses on the five human senses, which are sight, hearing, smell, taste, and touch, is also one of the key factors of neuromarketing. By understanding the five senses and trigger points, marketers can implement the insights into their marketing strategies to influence consumer purchasing behavior (Isa et al., 2019).

3.4.1 Neuromarketing and product design – *Packaging*

Neuromarketing applied to product packaging is of fundamental importance in the customer's purchasing decision. So not only the functionality and price but also the overall design affects whether the customer buys the given product or not. Various research and studies collect data on the impact of design products on the customer using biometric tests – eye tracking or facial analysis. They usually take place in a retail environment. Biometric testing has huge advantages as it can reveal customer reactions to packaging colors, shapes, symbols and product structure, and so on.

The advantages of the biometric test are easily applicable given that every person (regardless of culture, language, skin color, or gender, does not have to be a scientist or a marketer) can adopt the principles of neuromarketing through human factors (Müller, 2019). According to Favier, Celhay, and Pantin-Sohier (2019), package design is one of the factors that can influence brand perception and consumer purchase intention. The degree of simplicity in packaging design has a significant impact on brand perception, a simpler graphic design indicates a more successful image and is prone to higher purchase intention on the part of consumers. One example of a company is Apple. Apple takes simplicity as the main design principle when designing its packaging. Not only is their label prominent on the packaging, but it is also easy for consumers to remember.

Reimann et al. (2010) found that products with aesthetic packaging significantly increased the reaction time of consumers' choice responses and encouraged consumers to choose such products over well-known brands in standardized packaging, even if they were at a higher price.

According to Stoll et al. (2008), attractive packaging causes more intense activity changes in brain regions associated with positive emotions, reward, and impulsive and reflexive systems, whereas unattractive packaging causes less intense activity in these brain regions, activating areas of the brain associated with negative emotions. These findings imply that activating neural activity in brain areas involved with happy emotions, as well as impulsive and spontaneous processes, might predict significant impulse purchase tendencies.

3.4.2 Neuromarketing and price – *Pricing*

Price is a very important attribute in the success of selling a product. This area of the neuromarketing research process allows using EEG brain scans and psychophysiological measurements to find out how much consumers are willing to pay for a product and subsequently the sales strategy – it measures the willingness to pay. This investigation cannot predict the future behavior of the customer. The above can also be investigated in the form of questionnaires (Müller, 2019).

Karmarkar, Shiv, and Knutson (2015) found that overall evaluations of a product's monetary value (observed in altered activity patterns in the medial prefrontal cortex directly before a purchase decision) were higher when consumers were exposed to the price early. This can be useful in promoting the purchase of products at a good price when their value is easily recognized.

Somervuori and Ravaja (2013) produce similar results and emphasize the importance of emotional factors in price formation. Their study shows that low prices and national brand products stimulate higher positive emotions than high prices and private label products and also that positive emotion leads to greater purchase intentions.

3.4.3 Neuromarketing in advertisement

Nowadays, it is difficult to impress the customer with advertising, and quite often, we come across the concept of marketing smog. Marketing smog is a term used to describe the absorption of people by advertising. The goal is to interest the customer in a short time to buy the product. To attract the customer, the advertisement must be effective and, concerning the premises of the store, it should have the right location so that it has a strong, contrasting effect and does not blend in with the environment (Matúš, 2011). Neuroscientific methods explain the most differences in consumer emotions (e.g., increased emotion regulation in response to emotional appeals such as fear appeals) and in advertising elasticity or success (e.g., attention, affect, memory, desire) beyond basic traditional measures (e.g., traditional self-reports) (Barnett, Cerf, 2017).

Most brands on the market use neuromarketing, which is based on the evaluation of a person's hidden psychophysiological reactions, which change depending on the emotions experienced. Measuring emotions makes it possible to create an advertisement so that it is precisely targeted at the customer and can influence their purchasing behavior. They compile the advertisement based on data detected by medical devices, which monitor the change in brain and heart activity, muscle tension, breathing, temperature, and eye movement caused by the perception of the advertisement. Specialists in the field of marketing communication as well as clinical psychologists and sociologists agree that neuromarketing is very accurate and can save advertisers money invested (Matúš, 2011).

To move forward developmentally, future neuromarketing research should consider a deeper examination of the various neural pathways underlying advertising recognition and recall, as well as post-advertisement decision-making. In doing so, research should be able to shed more light on very promising areas in advertising, such as the contribution of different components and ad duration concerning the magnitude and salience of brand memories within the persuasive hierarchy (i.e., ads that provide information and reasons to purchase for the assumption of gradual mental processing) and reinforcement (i.e., the ongoing process of forming, changing and strengthening preferences) of advertising models (Plassmann et al., 2007).

The tobacco industry used neuromarketing after they had to deal with the ban on standard advertising. This type of promotion doesn't feel like advertising at all, yet it's so effective that, according to functional magnetic resonance imaging, it produces comparable activity in the part of the brain called the nucleus accumbens (dopamine receptors) associated with reward, cravings, and addiction to that of looking at a pack of cigarettes. The condition is that this visual stimulus lasts less than five seconds. Neuromarketing experts have found that if potential customers form a strong association between a product and a certain set of images, that are completely unrelated to the product, over time it is sufficient to present only these, seemingly unrelated stimuli. These subliminal attacks on our subconscious mind produce activity indicating that the urge to light a cigarette has been triggered, according to MRI scans of brain activity (Majba, 2018).

Neuromarketing tries to find out what interests the customer, what slogan, what colors, and the overall presentation. Customers must be cautious and not be misled by traders. Merchants often do not provide all information about the product, price, and conditions to influence purchasing behavior and obtain a large number of customers.

In connection with this procedure, the question arises as to how much neuromarketing in the field of advertising is ethical and in accordance with the law (Matúš, 2011).

3.5 Disadvantages of neuromarketing

Considering that there are important topics in marketing that are difficult to measure with neuroscientific methods, neuromarketing can only contribute to a small part of solving marketing topics.

There are survey methods for investigating purchase intention or loyalty that have been developed in the social sciences, but it is difficult to interpret how neuroscience can describe these constructs. Consumer loyalty is usually measured with repurchase intention, consumer recommendation, price sensitivity, and/or intention to purchase other products/services. Since neuroscientific methods can observe neural brain activity and capture feelings and emotions, the traditional perception of loyalty may change in the neuromarketing context, as the above variables cannot be measured by these medical devices. In addition, especially in consumer research, marketers have developed several models to describe consumer behavior in various fields to examine the relationship and effects between constructs developed in recent decades. Investigating the complex structures of these constructs can be quite difficult or even impossible (Huszár, Pap, 2016).

Because neuromarketing research requires interdisciplinary expertise, representatives from various disciplines, and specialized medical equipment, it is difficult to find market research companies that can accomplish such research. Universities where the necessary disciplines are represented and special medical devices are available may be suitable research partners for neuromarketing research. However, these institutions are fragmented, and due to the existing norms of academia (including teaching duties, open science norms, etc.) and lack of experience interacting with industry, research results may be too exploratory or scientific, which may have a high scientific value, but such results are hardly applied in practice (Huszár, Pap, 2016). Problem areas of concern in terms of neuromarketing research are shown in Figure 3.4.

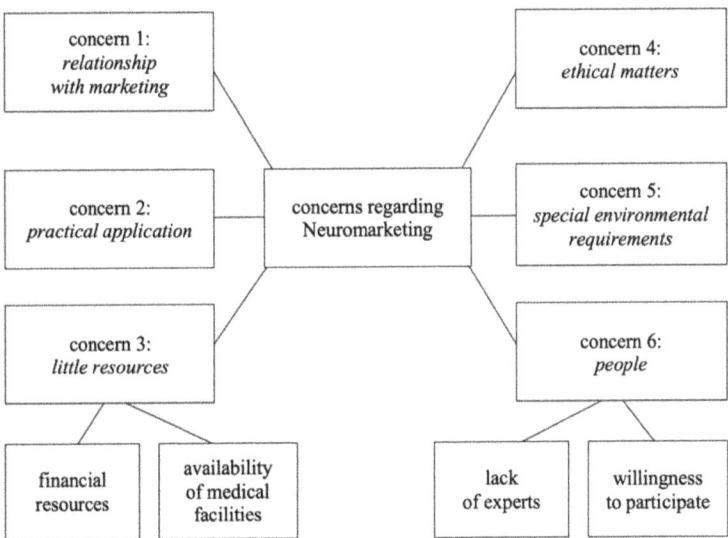

Figure 3.4. Concerns regarding Neuromarketing research
(*Source:* Huszár, Pap, 2016, pp. 165)

We distinguish two reasons that can hinder neuromarketing research: *factors influencing participation* and special environmental conditions. In certain examinations (such as Positron emission tomography), radioactive isotopes should be injected into the body intravenously to label specific molecules, which can deter participants from participating in research due to radioactive elements (even if it is medically safe) and cause injury to the participant. In addition, in some cases, participants have to take off their clothes and accessories, which is also uncomfortable and strange during marketing research. All these factors can reduce participants' willingness to participate in neuromarketing research (Huszár, Pap, 2016).

Courbet and Benoit (2013) criticize researches that although they are useful from a scientific point of view and describe interesting phenomena, they do not bring any benefit to marketing communication, nothing usable in practice. They criticize Knutson's experiment (Knutson et al., 2007), in which a person desires a product and the moment he learns its price, he is no longer interested in it. According to the authors, this does not need to be investigated using fMRI. According to them, this information can also be obtained using traditional methods and with much lower financial costs. Subsequently, they also criticize the conclusions of researches, which, according to them, have no benefit for marketing and are not applicable in practice.

4 Ethics of neuromarketing research

One of the biggest disadvantages of neuromarketing is the ethical dimension. Several authors claim that information captured by neuromarketing should be ignored, and its use in marketing campaigns should be prohibited (Huszár, Pap, 2016). According to Lee et al. (2007), these techniques are unacceptable because they enter consumers' opinions. While in the case of a survey with questions of a personal nature, it is possible to refuse to answer the questions, in the case of a brain test, this is not possible. The problem is that researchers capture more information from the test than the research purpose requires. Ethical issues deserve special attention because, during the investigation, researchers capture information that is not a part of the research, which can lead to invasion of privacy, for example, if the researchers discover medical disorders (e.g., brain tumor) in the participants. On the one hand, the researchers cannot determine what exactly it is, but it seems to be an anomaly, while on the other hand, the researchers were probably not trained and experienced in how to communicate this information to the research respondent (Huszár, Pap, 2016).

The issue of the ethics of neuropsychology of consumer behavior combines topics related to the research of consumer behavior in marketing and ethical topics associated with the study of the human brain. The ethical dimension of neuromarketing is one of the biggest and the most sensitive challenges in terms of its application in the field of market research. Since it emerged as a science, neuromarketing has caused many controversies and ethical issues among researchers. Such reactions are triggered by a research methodology that some authors believe has a great potential to reach the subject's mind.

The media's approach to neuromarketing reinforced people's mistrust of the new technology, as some media reports mentioned the discovery of a "buy button" in the human brain (Lindstrom, 2009).

To some extent, it would allow the brain of consumers to be tricked and manipulated into making purchasing decisions in favor of a particular company, product, or service. Neuromarketing has both *ardent proponents* and *straightforward skeptics*, just like any other new field. Neuromarketing advocates claim that it is advantageous for businesses and consumers since it will promote the creation of products that people want (Singer, 2004).

On the other hand, critics warn that people's ability to make informed decisions about purchases and (or) consumption will be compromised. Wilson (2008) and his colleagues address the ethical dimension of the impact of marketing (and recently also neuromarketing) actions on an individual's freedom of choice. They propose a model of persuasion that suits both traditional marketing actions, such as the development and implementation of promotional activities, as well as activities based on neuromarketing research. During the screening phase, the subject's brain activity is recorded using neuromarketing techniques, providing information about their subconscious reactions. The data is then analyzed to create a marketing message aimed at triggering the affective regions of the brain associated with pleasure and reward (Wilson et al., 2008). Neuromarketing research is currently conducted on well-defined samples that allow statistical validation of results. Current research creates the basis for the application of personalized marketing, which could be achieved by applying specific incentives for the individual (Foscht, Swoboda, 2011).

A serious dilemma facing researchers and companies willing to implement these models is the ethical nature of market research accomplished using neuromarketing techniques. With the traditional model, the potential invasion of the subject's privacy is that the subject is not fully informed about the subsequent use of the data collected during the screening phase. However, with the neuromarketing technique, the procedure is much more complicated. While confidentiality of brain activity data must be ensured, ownership rights to the recordings, rights for subsequent use, and distribution to third parties, must also be addressed (Wilson et al., 2008).

Neuromarketing research allows not only the identification of emotions evoked by a marketing message or a specific product but also the establishment of correlations between these emotions and message elements (or product characteristics). An ethical problem arises when this feedback is used to create a message aimed at increasing sales but which does not faithfully reflect the reality of the product's features (Wilson et al., 2008). It could mislead consumers into buying goods that do not meet their needs and do not live up to the promises made. The rules of ethical marketing categorically reject such practices. Moreover, it is believed that the economic success of such action depends explicitly on the trust that subjects place in neuromarketing research and its results (Brammer, 2004).

Another issue is consumer consent to constant tracking and exposure to marketing messages. For example, software programs that record and interpret an individual's facial expression and detect a consumer's emotions or reactions when standing in front of a product. This information is usually collected through video cameras installed in stores (Foscht, Swoboda, 2004). As a result, marketers collect information about consumers without asking their permission or even without informing them about it.

Another ethical concern for the use of neuroscientific methods in marketing involves scientific reliability, validity, and transparency. Of particular importance is the scientific competence of the marketing researcher who assumes the role of neuroscientist and the scientific quality of the neuroscientific method used to conduct neuromarketing research (Ulman et al., 2015).

More specifically, the interpretation of neuroscientific findings requires a high level of neuroscientific knowledge to appropriately mark the boundaries of possible outcomes and limitations of the use of the neuroscientific method in an effort to transparently communicate reliable, valid and meaningful interpretations of neuroscientific observations (Ulman et al., 2015).

Lack of competence can result in inaccurate reporting of marketing research advancements, under- or over-estimation of neuroscientific findings, and the creation and implementation of ineffective marketing tactics (e.g., backward inference, publication bias for positive results) (Plassmann et al., 2012).

The protection of research subjects is one of the ethical concerns in neuromarketing research. Particularly crucial topics are those involving informed consent, privacy, and vulnerability. More particular, it can endanger test participants' autonomy while measuring and mapping neurological responses to marketing stimuli in the human brain.

Although informed consent and privacy protection are among the necessary obligations that every researcher should ensure when conducting studies involving human subjects. The question of adequate protection afforded to test subjects in neuromarketing studies is often raised when neuroscientists do not take steps to obtain informed consent and protect their privacy (Murphy et al., 2008). These measures include information about study procedures, benefits and risks of study participation, test subjects' rights, types of findings that are obtained from them, and measures taken to ensure confidentiality and privacy (Slowther, Kleinman, 2009). The importance of such protection becomes more important for vulnerable groups such as children, patients, prisoners, and people (or their family members) with neurological diseases or psychological disorders, as these groups can be very vulnerable, easily deceived, or negatively affected by using neuroscientific technologies (Luna, Macklin, 2012).

Although the use of neuromarketing techniques and tools appears to be not only a simple task but also highly beneficial for a company that wants to promote a specific product, service or brand, thereby inducing favorable behavior from the targeted segment (preference, purchase, recommendation, etc.), from such an action entails great responsibility. It is mainly because, during the application of neuromarketing techniques, favorable or unfavorable manipulation of the client may occur. Therefore, the main challenge facing researchers in the field of neuromarketing and the difficulty of ethically implementing this procedure lies in assuring participants that their manipulation is positive, and pursuing rational educational goals beneficial to people and society. It should be about campaigns against drug addiction, smoking, excessive consumption of alcohol and sweets, unhealthy food, etc., and campaigns to promote a healthy lifestyle (Devaru, 2018).

The use of neuroscientific methods requires good ethical behavior in the planning and implementation of neuromarketing experiments, such as providing sufficient protection to test subjects; full disclosure of study objectives, risks, and benefits; procedures for informed consent; explicit protocols for addressing major and minor neuroscientific findings; and ethical review before the actual research (Murphy et al., 2008).

First of all, traders must be aware of which tools they will use to influence the customer's decision so that these do not conflict with good morals, the law, or ethical principles. It is important to approach each customer individually, to be aware of and adopt the basic principles of marketing communication, etc. A customer may perceive neuromarketing as a method of manipulating human thinking. In some cases, this is because it is difficult to prevent the misuse of this science, especially in the field of ethics. The results obtained using this method are not influenced by the prejudices of customers nor by their reluctance to reveal the truth. The problem arises when the results are damaged or misused by researchers. It is, therefore, necessary to take care of the autonomy of customers so that there is no violation of the law when it comes to research in the commercial sphere (Murphy et al., 2008).

5 Neurolinguistic Programming (NLP)

Richard Bandler was a psychology student and John Grinder was a professor at the University of California, Santa Cruz. Both of them initially performed research on the factors that contribute to an individual's excellence and his ability to reproduce it when necessary. They discovered through observation that the researched individuals expressed their thought and behavior tendencies. These patterns were recognized by Bandler and Grinder, who then developed a method known as Neurolinguistic Programming (NLP) to support them (Churches, West-burnham, 2008).

In order to develop a set of strategies for the things we do, such as making decisions, forming relationships, inspiring others, or coaching, neurolinguistic programming (NLP) studies how we think and behave. It is possible to learn how we think and act, what makes it possible for us to act in the ways we want to and obtain the results we deserve through the use of neurolinguistic programming, which may reach not only the conscious but also unconscious parts of our minds (Knight, 2015).

The roots of NLP go back to 1976 (the 70s of the 20th century). It was created by mathematics student Richard Bandler and speaker John Grinder. The two founders sought a pragmatic approach and modeled formulas that could be for common problems. They studied three personalities of Virginia Satir, Milton H. Erickson, and Fritz Perls, and they wanted to find out why they are smarter than the rest of their colleagues (Oupic, 2008).

In order to support both subjective and objective well-being, flexibility, and other abilities aimed at creating a satisfying life, Lubeck (1996) defined neurolinguistic programming as the systematic and effective use of every human being who is capable of remembering, forgetting, evaluating information, displaying it, and reacting to areas of a human being. We often encounter this term in psychology as a part of neuropsychological therapy. NLP is a process based on how specific abilities of a person can be transferred to another person so that the other person can use them practically. According to Lahnerová (2009), the acronym NLP stands for:

1. *Neuro*: the fundamental idea of NLP is based on the assumption that every behavior is based on neurological processes, and that every individual has a nervous system and communicates with the world through the senses.

2. *Linguistic*: indicates that we use language as the mean of our thoughts and behavior with the environment, an internal monologue about what we perceive, how we perceive and experience when communicating with people.
3. *Programming*: refers to possibilities that we can afford for the organization of our thoughts and ideas and actions to achieve results (repeating patterns of perception of thinking and feeling, our conscious and unconscious planning of the situation based on the linguistic evaluation of the perceived goal).

Neurolinguistic programming is a methodology founded on the active participation of an individual or group in their change. NLP manages its successful campaign in the environment of hundreds of methodologies focused on communication, health prevention, management, therapeutic practice, personal development, HR, management, and other areas thanks to its simplicity, comprehensibility, and efficiency affecting the entire personality of the individual at the level of identity. NLP makes it possible to carry out fundamental changes that affect a person's identity, support dynamics, and supplement it with new abilities (Dilts, 1996).

Neurolinguistic programming is a discipline that analyzes the individual perception of the world to increase people's success. NLP emphasizes both verbal and non-verbal communication. It examines the relationship between communication, the way of thinking (neuro), and behavior using various techniques for improving communication (linguistics) and changing behavior (programming) aimed at achieving a goal (Lahnerová, 2009).

Given the uncertainty covering certain workplace mental health initiatives, some companies have prioritized the use of neuro-linguistic programming (NLP) techniques to improve various occupational psychological outcomes, including job stress and self-esteem (Gray, Liotta, 2012; Wake, 2008). In addition, it is used by organizations to support goal setting, team building, self-management and leadership (Yamazaki, 2007). NLP helps professionals analyze how excellent the achieved results are and then determine how best to reproduce them (O'Connor, McDermott, 2001).

Although NLP seems to be well accepted in the management sector, the science of NLP has been criticized as being underdeveloped (Pensieri, 2013). Sturt et al. (2012) examined NLP in the context of health outcomes and concluded that much of the research was limited by major methodological issues (e.g., failure to state goals, interventions, etc.). Additionally, other literature reviews highlighted issues regarding researchers' misunderstanding of the essence of NLP (Pensieri, 2013). However, despite this criticism, there is an evidence-based understanding of the first-hand experiences of managers who have completed NLP training.

NLP often uses expressions such as there is no failure, only feedback, or there is a positive intention behind every behavior (O'Connor, Mcdermott, 2001). These assumptions, following the example of excellent communicators, are pedagogic tools to help practitioners make internal changes as a result, clients or staff reevaluate assumptions, thoughts, and behaviors (Grimley, 2013). So we can say that the function of NLP is to challenge or change mental frameworks (Rosen, 1991). As a result, NLP techniques can offer managers more supportive and motivational leadership styles in reframing their way of thinking and relationships with employees (Dilts, 1996).

Most managers prefer to refer to the practice as coaching and the term NLP tends to take a back seat. This is consistent with the wider perception of NLP among professional organizations and suggests that coaching is a more accepted term than NLP. For example, coaching psychology was recognized by the British Psychological Society (BPS) in 2004 (BPS, 2022), whereas NLP has not yet been officially recognized. This is even though there are significant overlaps between NLP and coaching in terms of their theoretical foundations and techniques of use (McDermott, Jago, 2006). In addition, coaching is regulated by the International Coaching Federation, but there is currently no established regulatory body for NLP (Grimley, 2016). Coaching could also be considered commercially available, as it involves more frequent license renewals than NLP.

A problem in NLP can be the reticence of some people or employees when discussing emotions at work. This may be due to gender differences, culture, and the fact, that some people feel considerable shame when discussing mental health issues (Tanaka et al., 2003). Neurolinguistic programming is relevant for direct forms of sales, but it is also applicable in marketing, for example, advertising. NLP prefers an individual approach because people respond more to direct contact, that is, they respond to one of their senses – – visual and auditory. People also process information subconsciously. NLP, which dates back to 70 years ago, has many features in common with the development of neuromarketing. Neuromarketing examines the human brain in reactions to advertising, for example. There are studies and research that have concluded that neuromarketing and neurolinguistic programming are effective methods that evaluate customer decisions (Agrawal, 2016).

It is defined as a model of interpersonal communication and an alternative approach to psychotherapy. It is based on the language study, communication, and personality changes. It is a set of techniques, axioms, and opinions used as the rule, an approach to personal development. This model is built on the basic idea that the mind, body, and language interact to create each person's perception of the world and that these perceptions, along with behavior, can be changed using various techniques. According to Lahnerová (2009), NLP is built on four pillars:

1. Result: setting out in advance the result we want to achieve.
2. Observer: discovering and recognizing important facts around the observer.
3. Flexibility: according to the acquired knowledge, it is necessary to adjust one's behavior flexibly.
4. Evaluation of reports: evaluation of overall knowledge and concluding.

Knight (2015) states that neuro-linguistic programming is concerned with how to achieve unique results and how to excel. Gradually, he finds more and more methods and tools based on which we can reveal and get to know the factors that enable us to be excellent. It involves modeling unique, specifically human, conscious, as well as unconscious, patterns of thinking, communication, and behavior. Because it is based on knowledge of what works, particularly what works well, neurolinguistic programming differs from conventional approaches. Each person uses particular terms and puns to refer to a particular sensory system, whether it is visual, auditory, or kinesthetic (sometimes olfactory or gustatory). Three representative systems of communication channels are distinguished by NLP (Lahnerová, 2009):

- visual,
- audio,
- kinesthetic system.

While psychotherapy also entered the training of managers, businessmen, and other professionals who need to improve their communication skills with people, NLP entered effective communication and is one of the alternative psychotherapy methods, which is why it is still a well-known and effective communication technique today. These behavioral systems allow to determine the most effective ways to communicate with customers (Lahnerová, 2009).

The importance of understanding innovative methods to use new technologies is the significance of neurolinguistic programming. We won't get new results if we just keep doing what we've been doing.

5.1 Neurological levels

The author of the logical model, respectively the neurological level, is R. Dilts (1998). The concept is based on NLP. All processes and elements of a person's subjective experience can be organized according to levels that influence each other. It is an effective tool that will help a person to find blocks, convictions, and beliefs in themselves that are holding them back from fluency. A higher level can effectively change and influence a lower level always. Conversely, a change at a lower level can rarely effectively change a higher level.

Dilts (1998) created an elegant model for thinking about personal change, learning, and communication. It also forms the context for thinking about NLP techniques. It presents a framework for organizing and gathering information, making it easier to determine the best point for intervention to achieve the desired change. We don't change in small or large parts, we change organically. The question is where to push to create a different desired result? Learning and change can take place at different levels. We can imagine the model of neurological levels as a pyramid with six floors. Let's take a look, from top to bottom, at what's on each floor:

5.1.1 Surrounding

It is a static level that describes a person's environment, social circle, interests, and everyday experience. It is a space in which human behavior is manifested. It rarely happens that a change of environment changes a person's behavior, activities, and rituals. The questions that a person needs to ask themselves in this situation are: Where and when am I like this? Who does this happen to me most often? In what situations? Or simply questions: What? Who? Where?

5.1.2 Behavior

It is the level of human interaction with the environment, change, and movement. Mostly it's about what a person does and doesn't do. It is about what one can see and hear. It is about everything that a person does when communicating – movements of hands, feet, and face. The individual is often not aware of it at all. It is necessary to identify what we do. It is important to observe yourself. The questions that a person needs to ask themselves in this situation are: How do I look? Where am I looking if I look away? What movements do I do? Or simply the question: What does it do?

5.1.3 Abilities and skills

A person can change, which is limited only by the change in the technology available to that person. A person needs to ask these questions in this situation: Under what circumstances am I able to be different? Am I aware that I can be different? Or simply questions: How?

5.1.4 Values and beliefs

A deep and structured level is responsible for a person's internal motivation. It is the core of the personality, formed around the tenth year of a person's life, and is very difficult to change. However, changes at the level of beliefs strongly affect all lower levels. Beliefs are often opinions about ourselves. It's a learned way of thinking. Beliefs are either created by ourselves or taken from someone else. So it does not mean that it is also a reality. Questions a person needs to ask himself in this situation: Am I convinced that I can be different? Do I believe that I will be the way I am for the rest of my life? How do I know that? Where does this belief come from? Or simple question: Why?

5.1.5 Identity (mission)

It is a personality level that describes who a person feels like they are in a global sense. These are 'stickers' that a person adopted or just put on himself. This level talks about how a person perceives himself and how others perceive him. It is closely related to the previous level: I am what I believe. In the first case, we evaluate the behavior, in the second case, we give ourselves a label, an identity. By accepting it unconsciously, it affects all of one's beliefs about who one is. Questions a person needs to ask himself in this situation are: How do I perceive myself? What role do I identify with? How do others perceive me? What do I want to be? Or simply the question: Who am I?

5.1.6 Connection (mission, transmission, meaning)

There is a spiritual level that goes beyond the vision of one's personality, something elusive. It is about the highest meaning and purpose of man. It is a relationship with something higher that transcends man. It is a connection with family, company, community, god, and spirituality. This perception is influenced by culture or religion. This includes what I pass on to the people around me. The questions a person needs to ask themselves in this situation are: How will what I do affect my surroundings? How will this situation help my surroundings and my family?

Within the neurological levels, it is important to answer all the questions and identify the challenges that one needs to work on. Each of these descriptions looks at the situation from a different point of view. Together, however, they give a comprehensive view on which a person can build and understand the functioning of this process. A person can find a way to eliminate what negatively affects him (Zamfir et al., 2013).

Successful managers draw information from within themselves: it is their own and unique, and create their formula for success. However, it is not enough for them to believe they can be excellent managers – they need to strengthen their belief with work, skills, and behavior. It will allow them to create their own pattern of success. They need to find out how to learn from every person, every situation, and every knowledge. The ability to manage one's thoughts, emotions, actions, conflicts, and experiences, determines whether someone becomes a leader who leads others to creative cooperation. The pyramid of neuro-logical levels helps to achieve these abilities, which is extensive, and it is up to each manager how he will use it (Tomašovič, 2015).

5.2 Communication patterns based on NLP

The brain together with the nervous system can be programmed. NLP techniques help to choose the right words, ways of thinking, and actions leading to the goal we set. NLP techniques represent a modern way to become a successful businessman, manager, or seller who will be able to reach an agreement with other people (customers) (Rebeťák, 2016). According to Rebeťák (2016), NLP communication techniques can be formulated into the following formulas:

5.2.1 Mind reading

A technique based on which we monitor the customer's non-verbal communication and use the experience of the behavior of other customers (probable thoughts that may be going on in the customer's mind). Formula: You may be thinking about etc. Example: Maybe at this moment you can't decide what (which product) to choose.

5.2.2 Agreeable attitude

One of the best formulas that we use in situations where it is necessary is to weaken the customer's defenses and force him to listen. Formula: I agree, and I would add that, etc. Example: Of course, it is not appropriate to agree with what you disagree with, and I would add that you can only agree with that part of the opinion with which it is possible to agree.

5.2.3 A sequence of several affirmative statements or questions

A technique in which, by using several expressions or statements of agreement, the customer naturally agrees with the last formulated request (statement) of the seller. A very effective technique for responding to customer rejection. The formula: Do we agree that etc.? And also etc.? We can agree on etc. X and Y are the things on which there is an agreement, and the customer answers YES. Z is the thing you want from the customer. Example: You have been coming to us for a long time, and you have been satisfied so far, we tried to accommodate you, and we will certainly resolve the situation now.

5.2.4 Hyptnotic accompanying and guidance

A technique based on sensory verifiable and demonstrable statements that are true, the customer subconsciously agrees with the stated fact. Then when the seller adds something provable that you want the customer to believe, it becomes easier to convince them.

5.2.5 Breaking the formula with NLP

The basic principle behind this technique is that salespeople like a coherent sequence of ideas, thoughts, or events. If this pattern is disturbed, there will be some confusion, which can lead to a sudden trance. The formula can be used effectively in response to unreasonable or unauthorized customer requests. Formula: Unexpected reaction..., A statement/command that directs the customer to what you want to happen. Example: Then go to buy it somewhere else! Look, we are reasonable people, and we will solve this situation.

5.2.6 Reporting negative things

The essence of this technique is that the negative information is announced at first, then a positive sentence is added to the negative information with the conjunction BUT. The conjunction BUT deletes what has been said so far, so the addressee can accept and listen to what we say next. Example: We do not have this product available, but we can order it for you, and you can have it within a few days.

5.2.7 The pattern of awareness in NLP

This formula includes the words notice, realize, experience, understand, and be aware – words describe thinking processes in the customer's mind. These are very effective because we assume that everything that follows them is true. When a declarative sentence is transformed into an interrogative one, the power of the formula increases. For example: As you read these sentences, you begin to notice how effective the pattern of awareness is.

Communication patterns based on NLP can also be manipulative. There is a very fine line between manipulation and motivation. We find that after communication if the customer benefits from the conversation and gives a positive opinion, we talk about motivation. If the opposite scenario occurs, we are talking about manipulation. There is one more fundamental thing in business behavior. If a customer receives something from which he does not benefit, he may get the feeling that he was manipulated and visit another seller a second time (Rebeťák, 2016).

5.3 NLP techniques

A series of effective techniques, tools, and exercises help an individual to achieve a goal focused on any area of life. NLP methodologies can not only thoroughly analyze, but also find solutions and keep them in the human nervous system.

NLP is known as the study of human perfection because NLP not only studies the most effective behaviors to achieve perfection but also explores the study of behavior, language, mental processes, and ways of thinking. This methodology is called NLP modeling. NLP has modeled many great figures in history to further model, report, and guide them, such as Virginia Satire, Fritz Perl, Milton Erickson, Aristotle, Sherlock Holmes, and Walt Disney (Dilts, 1994).

It is important to note that NLP is subjective and therefore cannot be evaluated as normal scientific research material. NLP is result-oriented and allows the organization to experience the result, at least as fantasy, so the motivation creates itself. The amazing methodology, Mind to muscle, is known (Hall, 2001). It's like transmitting places in the brain to make the legs follow – that is, the mind-muscle connection.

It says that when you experience the concept of mind, you feel that you want it so badly that you get cravings until a behavior or action is created. It also works on the principle of the foot forward phenomenon. An HR professional can be highly effective by experiencing an increase in efficiency using this method and in this way achieve excellence in employment. It also enables employees to remove traditional limiting beliefs by challenging them with 'what if I can' then imagining 'as if it could' (Dilts, 1994).

All this is possible with the help of various NLP techniques such as mind mapping, metaprogramming, stress management, brain gymnastics, and the Disney model of creativity.

5.3.1 Mind mapping

Mind mapping is a technique developed by Tony Buzan in the 1960s. It is a powerful graphic technique that provides a universal key to unlocking the brain's potential. Mind maps were designed based on research into how our brain works.

According to Hamdyi et al. (2009), the advantages of using mind maps include:

- accelerate learning capacity,
- reveal connections and links between different subjects,
- develop effective brainstorming techniques,
- help the mind to become a powerful generator of ideas,
- provide insight into the overall picture of any project,
- increase the ability to remember and remember.

Mind maps can be applied to every aspect of life where better learning and clearer thinking will increase human performance. Creating mind maps manually, takes a long time and requires a lot of effort. Automatizing the creation of mind maps is a better solution that gives privileges without the trouble of creating them (Saelan, Purwarianti, 2013).

5.3.2 Braingym

According to Ibrahim (2011), the reduction of depression in humans can be done through the use of pharmacology, namely antidepressants. Another theory states that non-pharmacological therapy such as color therapy, music therapy, aromatherapy, and Brain Gym (Yanuarita, 2012) can be used to reduce depression in humans, which involves cleansing the brain (eliminating negative thoughts, envy, addiction), improving breathing, endurance training, tension release, reduction of fatigue, improvement of inattention, and lack of concentration. With the help of brain gymnastics, depression can be eliminated in people who have negative thoughts and behave without inspiration, lack concentration, and do not perform daily activities. Subsequently, they can be motivated again to satisfy their physical and psychosocial needs (Dennison, et al., 2009). Yanuarita (2012) states that brain gymnastics can not only accelerate the flow of blood and oxygen to the brain, but it can optimally stimulate the work and function of the brain, which means activating the abilities of the right and left hemispheres to establish cooperation between them. Brain gymnastics will also increase the quality of people's lives (Pragholapati, 2019).

Various studies prove that brain exercise is fun, easy, and suitable for everyday activities because it can be done at any time and anywhere and can improve brain health.

5.3.3 Disney's creative strategy

The Disney NLP strategy is one of the techniques modeled by Robert Dilts using NLP. This technique is based on Walt Disney's excellence, bringing new ideas for animated films from fantasy to reality. Studies show that Disney NLP strategy can solve people's anxiety-related problems (Dilts, 1998).

The Disney NLP strategy was founded by Walt Disney in the production of creative animations. This strategy was modeled in 1994 by an NLP expert already mentioned, Robert Dilts (Dilts, 1994). The strategy includes three processes, namely creative, realistic and critical. All three of these processes are necessary to solve existing problems and find effective solutions. This process is called imagining (Dilts, 1998).

The Disney NLP strategy is, therefore, suitable for solving problems, especially in mathematics and natural sciences (Bell, 2016). The strategy differs from the sixth hat created by Edward De Bono (De Bono, 2017). The Disney NLP strategy emphasizes the irregularity of the process, starting with creative, realistic, and ending with critical, while the Six Thinking Hats technique does not emphasize rules. The Disney NLP strategy not only involves a cognitive process that thinks creatively, logically, and critically, but also involves controlling emotions (Bell, 2016).

A study conducted by Bell (2016) found that the Disney NLP strategy was able to reduce people's anxiety and make them happier. This is because the Disney NLP strategy uses this communication with oneself to influence the mind system to change needed emotions and thoughts.

Walt Elias Disney was an outstanding American businessman, producer, director, screenwriter, stuntman, animator, and philanthropist. The company he founded is now called The Walt Disney Company and is known in the world of management primarily for the method of managing the creative process called the Disney Creativity Strategy. Disney retained a technique adopted by coaching. With its use, we can be as creative as possible, see things in reality, and at the same time look for new solutions. It is suitable for planning in work and personal life. The method is based on the assumption that every person is partly a dreamer, realist, and critic, while each role includes a specific type of thinking and action (Ball, 1988; Podaná, 2012):

1. *Dreamer* – presents extraordinary and unusual scenarios for new business projects. For a Dreamer, every idea is possible because he wants it. He cannot invent nonsense, only perfect dreams that he would like to live out by himself. He can immerse himself in his imagination, where he excludes all distracting elements.
2. *Realist* – has a phenomenal ability to motivate and coordinate teams of different workers and breathe life into their dreams. It brings practical thinking and energy, but without it, it would be impossible to realize success, and only a flash of an idea would remain in the framework of dreaming. If our dream of what we would like and how it could work in an ideal world is complete, a Realist comes to the fore. The task of the realist is to make sure that the dream becomes a reality. A realist does not decide that some things are impossible but decides what can be done to make everything work. It looks for concrete steps to fulfill the plan and then finds out if the plan was fulfilled. To have enough information in his work, he must communicate with a dreamer who refines dreams and brings them closer to reality.
3. *Critic* – subjects every part of the work to strict control and criticism. It provides valuable feedback and tries to point out the real risks of failure. The critic does not judge the initial idea but only the implementation plan itself.

Disney's approach to creativity is not limited to animated feature films but is a strategy that leads to success in any creative endeavor. However, any creative project must contain all three aspects: creative imagination, practical activities, and critical refinement. The Disney method allows you to look at things from three different points of view, it shows how to fulfill your dreams, create visions, and how to plan them. If the vision is completely clear and the steps are realistic, and under control, miracles happen (Capodagli, Jackson, 1998).

5.3.4 The six thinking hats model

De Bono's model includes six different colored hats. Each hat represents a different way of dealing with critical thinking about how to approach and solve a problem.

The black hat is used for caution in critical thinking. De Bono chose black for careful critical thinking, as the word critical has its origin in Greek, meaning judge. De Bono (1992c) explains that in many countries, judges wear black, and therefore, black is appropriate for this way of thinking because it represents serious consideration of issues or problems to be solved. Problems include questioning the feasibility of alternative approaches to problem-solving, evaluating current problems, identifying what is wrong, finding weaknesses in an argument or proposal, and evaluating problems to make a judgment. Although the black hat is associated with thinking that questions and checks the feasibility and validity of propositions and seeks to evaluate and make judgments, it does not represent contradictory or undesirable thinking. It is not a bad hat. Critical thinking and problem solving while wearing a black hat create an opportunity to assess possible consequences of our decisions and save us the cost of implementing dysfunctional strategies or embarking on disastrous actions.

Wearing a blue hat brings the perspective of organizational critical thinking and metacognition. This makes blue hat thinking different from all other hats because while other hats are concerned with thinking about how to solve a particular problem, blue hat thinking focuses on thinking that will lead to a solution. Thus, blue hat thinking brings higher-order thinking to the process of critical thinking and problem solving, which involves active control over the cognitive processes involved in finding a reasonable solution to a problem. It helps to identify strategies and plan activities that can be implemented to solve the given problem.

We can associate the blue hat with the blue sky, which is above everything. If we were up in the sky, we could look down to see what happens on the ground below. With a blue hat, we try to rise above the thinking that is going on and gain insight into that thinking. With a blue hat, we try to take responsibility for our thinking to organize what is happening. (De Bono, 1992b) Thus, blue hat thinking brings a special perspective on critical thinking and problem solving that helps to define and formulate the nature of the problem, and set clear goals or objectives to be followed in solving this problem. Identifies alternative steps to take in finding a solution, evaluates and re-evaluates progress, and makes ongoing decisions about the next steps as progress is made toward the planned outcome.

The green hat is for creative critical thinking and problem-solving. We can look at the word creative in two ways. The first way means to generate, produce, and create something that was not there. The second way means having new ideas, new ideas, and ideas that have not been used before. In justifying the color green for this hat, De Bono (1992a) says that the color green evokes images of nature and vegetation, and therefore, green can easily symbolize productive capacity and energy tied up in natural resources. It brings to the process of critical thinking and problem solving new ideas, possibilities, suggestions, and proposals that have not been offered before. It, therefore, represents creative and innovative thinking. It is about moving forward to possibilities and new ideas (De Bono, 1992b).

The red hat brings opportunities for expressing personal emotions to the process of critical thinking and problem-solving. They express themselves without fear of being judged and without the need to apologize. Emotions, feelings, hunches, and intuitive ideas are shared in the context of free speech. Participants are free to say what they think about the approach being taken in trying to solve a problem at a particular time without having to provide an explanation or give reasons for their feelings. Since there is freedom of expression and no justification is needed, participants are free to express their feelings without having to look for logic and rationalization for those feelings. Emotions, feelings, premonitions, and intuitions are hidden under the red hat. The emotions that this hat brings to the thought process include joy, fear, anger, jealousy, and sadness. Feelings are broader than emotions (uncertainty, anxiety, likes, dislikes, interest, excitement), and intuitions are even broader than feelings (when a person acts instinctively, without rationalizing their actions). In essence, red hat thinking helps answer the question: What do I think about this? (De Bono, 1992c).

White hat thinking brings into the process of critical thinking and problem solving the information requirements that are needed to solve the problem. It focuses on 3 questions: What information do we have? What information do we need? How do we get the information we need? (De Bono, 1992b). Once we identify the information we need, white hat thinking allows us to go out and collect that information. This perspective includes both personal and group information seeking. De Bono associates this type of thinking with the white hat metaphor because he associates information with a typical report that provides information on white paper. It also refers to information in computer printouts, which are normally produced on white paper. Another association that De Bono makes with the color of this hat is newspaper information, which is again commonly printed on white paper. He extends his rationale for associating the color white with information by suggesting that whiteness signifies the neutrality and objectivity of the information sought by wearing this hat since all this hat seeks is information, without suggestions, ideas, or arguments.

Yellow hat thinking brings a sense of optimism and determination to succeed in the process of critical thinking and problem-solving. He looks for the strengths that we have and the opportunities that the situation offers. It seeks to draw on current strengths and achievements to advance to new heights of success. Current success drives the courage for further success. With this hat, alternative options are identified that can lead to improved performance. De Bono (1992b) says this involves looking for four aspects: the good points, the benefits, the reasons why the idea will work, and the likelihood of success. De Bono (1992c) links this optimistic approach to problem-solving to the color yellow, as it can represent sunshine and optimism and seeing the bright side of things. This optimism is based on supporting evidence and is not mere fantasy or wishful thinking driven by emotion.

5.3.5 NLP metaprograms

We characterize them as hidden strategies that take place in the background of a person's consciousness. It is a way of thinking and acting that we consider our own, but in its essence, it is a template that our organism uses without our consent and awareness in the case of a specific situation. Metaprograms deprive us of control over our thinking and behavior at a given moment, so we can say they are very dangerous thought processes. It is not easy to get rid of such thinking and behavior, even if we admit that our behavior is strange in certain situations or beyond our control, whether based on repeated experience or warnings from those around us. We can plan, rightly or wrongly, and eventually make wrong decisions at the last minute (Dilts, 2014).

It is like an automatic pilot that takes control of life for us without our knowledge and consent, and before we know it – we have lost. Standard metaprograms, as described in NLP manuals, can serve managers to make excellent use of the weaknesses and strengths of the people in their company. From a therapeutic and human point of view, any metaprogram is destructive because it deprives a person of contact with intuition, values, plans, goals, and people with whom one surrounds oneself. Metaprograms also arise as defensive psychological reactions in times of stressful situations. Stress has three basic forms, namely attack, flight, and passivity. Almost everyone has developed a pattern of reactions to stressful situations, which often work for us, even when we are no longer stressed. Auxiliary reactions move to the subconscious and control our emotions, thoughts, evaluations, and muscles (Furduescu, 2019).

Metaprograms operate in a wide range of human life whether it concerns approaches to work (a picky eater – visionary, freedom – necessity, external – - internal, etc.) or in the context of the wrong choice of partner, wrong choice of employees, investments, fear of certain decisions, low self-confidence, etc. Working with metaprograms requires identifying which of the neurological levels the program operates on. Removing the metaprogram can be done in all sorts of ways, but, almost always, it requires working with someone who sees us and our thought processes from the outside because the metaprogram is like an aquarium – we see outside but don't know we're inside. A fish in an aquarium, he does not know that he is a fish and that he is in an aquarium. Even a person caught in the energy of a metaprogram does not know that he is implementing a metaprogram (Knight, 2004).

They are often used as a motivational tool, suggesting a detailed hierarchy of what might motivate an individual when committing to an action. They propose a macro strategy, a marko program. These strategies include other strategies. Triggers of human metaprogram behavior have been identified, including areas of privileged interest, registers of understanding, motivation triggers, attitudes to change, metaphorical beliefs, action orientation, and decision systems. Each individual has metaprograms set in a certain way, thus, it requires different approaches and metaprograms (Furduescu, 2019).

5.3.6 Reframing

Before defining the term, it is necessary to mention that the terms frame and framing refer to the perspective from which one sees the world, the perspective, born from personal or environmental experiences. A person gives meaning to it according to his beliefs, values, and things he likes or dislikes. In other words, it represents the meaning that a person gives to the situation. When an individual has a pleasant experience, he does not like the reaction to the experience. There is nothing wrong with frames that an individual uses in different situations, except when a certain frame causes problems. The way the individual changes the response shows that the response itself is not based on what is happening in the sensory experience but on the interpretation. An individual tends to form beliefs, values, and things based on how he has perceived them in the past. Mostly, changing the usual norms of perception creates more life possibilities. If we look at the given situation from a different perspective, a person can change the way he reacts in life, his representation or perception, his state, behavior, and actions. This is about reframing. Reframing is the art and science of arranging words and actions to change one's perspective or another person's perspective in a particular situation to initiate a behavior change (O'Connor, McDermott, 2001).

Reframing is based on the assumption that none of our behavior is wrong, just sometimes inappropriate in a certain situation. The goal of reframing is to achieve desired behavior in the given situation.

We are talking about two strategies: we want to eliminate a certain behavior or we want to get a certain behavior. And so, for a satisfactory result, we need to eliminate inappropriate behavior (phobias, snoring, fear) or acquire some skills (presence skills, self-control, joy in life). But beware, removing your fear of water does not make you a great swimmer, or removing your fear of driving does not make you a great driver. After the removal of the phobia, fear, or block, it is important to check your satisfaction with the new state and possibly supplement or train other required skills. But even by removing the financial side metaprogram, we will not gain the ability to make the right strategic decisions and make the right investments. This is already a matter of professional training, knowledge of the market, but also luck (Dilts, 2014).

The main purpose of reframing is to define intentional behavior. In fact, reframing tries to give the same situation a new, different meaning. The purpose of the method is to transform the original meaning into a different one and move it into a new frame. There are two forms of reframing: contextual reframing (which can be defined as an experience that generates different consequences for the context of speech) and content reframing (refers to the fact that its goal is not to change contexts but to change perspectives that a person uses, making behavior more flexible and it is faster adapting to various changes in the organization) (Dilts, Lozier, 2000).

Special emphasis should be placed on employee motivation, as it has been found that hired staff, when motivated at work, tend to complete tasks much faster and with higher quality, leading to higher performance, lower employee turnover, and absenteeism. In most private organizations, the motivational system is quite functional, but in public organizations, this system, and especially the employee compensation system, is established by law, which makes it difficult to achieve employee motivation. Many steps are taken to improve the motivational system and to achieve the goals of public organizations at a good time, but we also have to reckon with compromises in the relationship between the employer and the employee (Dilts, 2008).

6 Factors in NLP and business

Mental manipulation in business behavior is for the seller to motivate the customer to buy. It is emotions that influence buyers' purchasing behavior. There is a connection of certain feelings with the selected product or service, and this, let's say that anchor, does not allow us to leave the product in the store. Emotion forces the buyer to buy because if he does not buy, the given emotion does not appear. The task of salespeople is to evoke the greatest and strongest possible optimistic emotion in the customer (customer interest) and induce desire and its direct connection with the offered product or service. It is exactly the form of mental (mind) manipulation that sellers deal with, as well as marketing itself (Hloušková, 2016).

Emotions and emotional intelligence are currently associated mainly with leadership, or the power to lead other people. Research shows that development and emotional intelligence are very significant sources of competitiveness. If the potential of emotional intelligence that lies in each of us is released and properly used in practice, it brings positive results in leading people. Developing emotional intelligence is a long-term and difficult process. Classical educational methods do not work in an emotional world. These facts, which have their evolutionary causes, mean that we rarely encounter the practical use of emotional intelligence in business behavior and the corporate environment (Hloušková, 2016).

Borgo (2006) states that several effective tools, or more or less proven theories of neurolinguistic programming, do not belong exclusively to it and have not been empirically proven. According to the author, the NLP does not provide any explanation at the neural level and is gaining popularity only because it is well promoted.

Briers (2012) says that NLP is not a coherent treatment but the content of different techniques without a precise theoretical basis. The author claims that NLP is narcissistic, self-centered, and detached from notions of responsibility.

Witkovski (2012) argues that the system of NLP techniques is predetermined to achieve personal success. According to the author, research in NLP has not been confirmed or denied by research and ends with indeterminate results. The research was focused on a very narrow group of problems. Hypnosis researcher Weitzenhoffer (1989) criticizes the approach of NLP founders in that their strong claims are based on untested hypotheses supported by absolutely insufficient data.

However, we think that NLP is the study of human excellence, which deals with ways to imitate and model this excellence. We accept the enormous complexity of human biology and the influence of the environment on it, just as NLP accepts each individual as unique for a given life path and situation. Therefore, it is appropriate to study this issue precisely in connection with business and emphasize each person's individuality.

6.1 Cognitive-emotional-behavioral factors in NLP

Neurolinguistic programming is one of the possible ways to improve the level of one's emotional intelligence and how to use this intelligence relatively quickly in practice when communicating with others. Numerous companies in the world use neuro-linguistic programming and NLP tools. We also find their use in the management literature (Hloušková, 2016).

Neuro-linguistic programming has countless tools to communicate with our limbic system. Therefore, the NLP is considered one of the effective means for developing emotional intelligence. Emotions in neurolinguistics are apprehended as psychological and physiological reactions to some stimulus, most often sensory stimulus. They cause affective reactions (subjective feelings), bodily reactions, and cognitive reactions. Together they form a system. It follows from the above that emotions have an impact on the overall person's state. However, it is possible to influence emotions with other components of the human personality. People let their emotions control them, e.g., in tantrums or expressions of enthusiasm. Suppressing emotions or letting them take over completely is an extreme solution. It is better and more effective to learn to work with emotions to work with other components of the human personality for the benefit of the given individual. As mentioned above, a sufficient level of the ability to work with emotions (emotional intelligence) is consequential for every person (Hloušková, 2016).

NLP is built on the communication skills of a specific person, on personal assumptions, values, beliefs, thinking, and the behavior itself. Its overall success depends on it.

6.1.1 Emotions as a mean of communication with the customer

Emotions represent the fastest means of communication. Sometimes words are not necessary. We believe that communicating properly is very important in business behavior. For example, a salesperson who communicates with a customer and wants to be successful in sales should be able to communicate effectively, know to control his emotions. Emotions contribute significantly to the power of communication. We use them to communicate effectively. Some emotions, as already mentioned, are given genetically, others socially learned. If we add an emotion expressing certain words, this expression has significantly more power. The basis is to be empathetic, to be able to manage your emotions, and empathize with the customer's emotions and with them to find out what their needs are (Koutná, 2017).

Customers pick up not only the words and intonation of spoken language but also body language; that is, they receive changes in physiology, in this case, emotions. According to some sources, body language and facial expressions make up to 38 % of received information. And what happens when a customer does not receive the information even though he expects it? Understandably, the customer is confused, and in the worst case, he suspects that it is not as the seller states, and in the worst case, he does not believe the information presented. It is important to communicate through all communication channels following what a successful salesperson or manager wants to say. And therefore also with the fastest means of communication – using emotions. What is the mission of marketing in this regard? Its task is not only to achieve profit but also to diversify the purchasing process – for sellers and customers. Thanks to marketing, sellers get closer to their customers and thus know their needs better and achieve communication, based on which they can evaluate their needs and improve their offers (Koutná, 2017).

Emotions affect us every day. They are used in marketing where we see the person as the emotional personality and the effect of marketing tools on the person. Emotions play a direct role in the unconscious and conscious decision-making process. Emotions are the central motivation for human behavior (Vysekalová, 2014).

Emotions also play a significant role in unconscious decision-making. According to Ohman's research, a group of people with various phobias (fear of spiders and snakes) was shown images of these animals for a short time. Participants did not register them consciously, but their physiological responses to these stimuli did. They accordingly confirmed the theory about the influence of emotions and unconscious stimuls on other processes in the body (Page, 2012).

6.1.2 Emotions as a decision-making support

Logically, customers can only make simple decisions, such as buying things, such as a toothbrush, soap, and hygiene items. In more complex matters, emotions are present that affect the rational decision-making process. It is difficult to impress the customer in the current competitive environment. The seller must be creative and come to the market with something that will interest the customer. There is a difference between what customers want and what they need. Most salespeople know that people are easily swayed by what they want. They are limited only by what they can afford. If a salesperson tries to recommend a specific product, they may perceive it as forcing. A better way is to show the product and provide information about it first. To know what information to communicate to the customer, the seller must learn to listen to the customer. Then, it depends on the customer to decide whether he will show interest in the product. Can you explain why the product is the one the customer wants? Why does he need it? Why should she long for him? (Koutná, 2017).

Technique and language patterns used by neurolinguistic programming describe the sentence: Words can be a weapon, act like a drug, and can lead us to wealth. We consider the influence on the customer's unconscious as the most important ability in business behavior. Figure 6.1 shows how specific parts of the human brain influence the customer's decision-making in shopping. The main thing is to remember that everything a good salesperson does and says will also affect the customer. People's behavior is predictable (Samuhelová, Šimková, 2015).

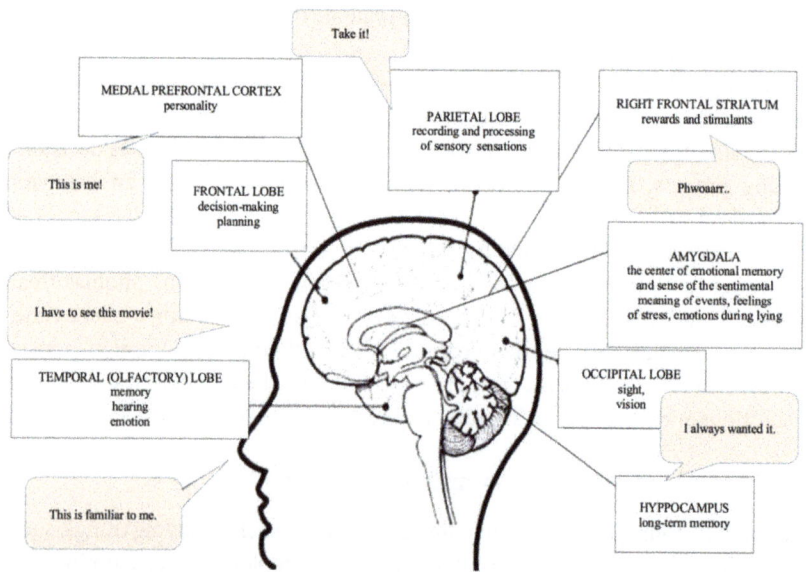

Figure 6.1. Parts of the brain that influence business behavior
(*Source:* Das, 2009)

It is marketing that encourages salespeople to pay more attention to customers and ultimately leave the decision up to the customer. Freeing yourself from the fear of emotions and meeting customers is one of the basic conditions for success in sales, as well as the success of top managers in leadership. In addition to performance as a leader, leadership personalities are also necessary. The leader is in the position of emotional leader for people who built trust in him and looked for emotional support and security. They expect their leader to provide them, among other things, with emotions, which he will then share with them. If this does not happen, they find someone else to lead them (Hloušková, 2016).

6.2 NLP as a tool of successful sales

The sale of specific products or services has the same rules, procedures, and laws. The basic element on which you can build and ruin a good sale is attracting the customer. The customer buys first of all from the seller and then what the seller sells (e.g., when selling over the phone). And that's why it is meant to impress the customer with an accurate communication form. NLP is a process that helps salespeople to develop and learn to communicate with customers and teaches how to effectively influence their thinking, so that it brings positive results in the given area (Gibson, 2011).

One of the applications of NLP is gaining the necessary self-confidence and successful communication with the customer. In the business sphere, NLP is valuable because it can affect consciousness. It is manageable to influence your thoughts, behavior, and emotions. It is important to remember what the customer says, what his needs are, and to satisfy them. The thought process leads us to the resulting behavior, but therefore, the main rule of successful sales is securing customers' trust. Figuratively speaking, people do not buy products mainly, but salespersons. Even a good sale will not take place without building trust since every activity is preceded by a thinking process (e.g., a certain decision is made before entering the store), and it is the thinking that leads to the resulting behavior of either sellers or customers (Gibson, 2011).

NLP in business behavior can extensively influence sales. It is necessary to think about particular rules to achieve success. The result is a successful business. Customers have their own methods, processes, and reasons for buying, and a good salesperson should be able to identify their needs within the first minutes of communication. According to Gibson (2011), a good salesperson finds:

- clients' purchase motivation,
- product expectations.

For these purposes, a special Behavioral & Language Model was created, based on NLP Metaprograms, used for a natural form with the customer. People buy based on emotions and make decisions based on fear, want, or curiosity. They do not buy houses, cars, or clothes because they need them but because they feel better – they fulfill their dreams with them. Logic and rational thinking come next. That is why it is so important to work with emotions and ideas. Correctly formulated questions and the art of using positive and negative emotions are the alpha and omega. The buyer perceives products and services offered by the seller as a goal. He buys them to fulfill his dream, to satisfy his needs. That is why many companies in the world, especially in the USA, use NLP to achieve their business goals. NLP is, therefore, used in large companies, as well as directly in sales and business (Gibson, 2011).

6.3 Main principles of NLP in managerial practice and business

The basic assumptions of NLP are rules observed in life, which have practical application in the practice of managers and entrepreneurs. They can be provocative in part because they challenge the excuses that allow us to stay where we are instead of growing and moving forward. Tomašovič (2015) includes among these principles:

6.3.1 Communication is continuous

We can communicate using our five senses – sight, hearing, touch, smell, and taste, the information is constantly passing through. Their evaluation takes place mostly without our awareness, and everyone within the range of communication is influenced by their message to a certain extent. When, for example, someone does not say anything during the discussion, he transmits the center of gravity of active communication to the accessible communication channels of the remaining four.

6.3.2 The meaning of communication is the reaction it generates

Whether the understanding works can be verified by the extent to which the recipient is able to understand what the sender wants on the information received. If this is not possible for him, however good the sender's intention may be, the recipient does not get anything out of it. The message must be tailored in such a way that the receiver is motivated to behave as the sender wishes. Otherwise, the communication will not achieve the intended benefit.

6.3.3 People react to their idea and model of reality, not to reality itself

If you had told someone 400 years ago about electric lights, airplanes, or cars, they would probably have laughed at you or brought you before the Inquisition. Today, these things are so commonplace and self-evident that no one stops to think about them. The generally mentioned picture of the world, our map of reality has changed and, consequently, people's reactions to certain things. Today, many people have a problem with the idea that immaterial forces are a reality and can affect a person's state of health. Paradoxically, nobody doubted it 400 years ago.

6.3.4 Body, spirit, and soul are different, closely connected partial aspects of the whole person. Changing one part affects the others

You must have registered that when something good happens to a person, you also have seen a change in his physical body – he has a straight posture, more forceful gestures, an enthusiastic facial expression, and shining eyes. In the same way, physical injury can fill a person's soul with fear and limit their logical judgment. The latest modern psychotherapy methods use these connections to heal their clients.

6.3.5 The most flexible person wins

If you bind yourself to certain ways of behavior when dealing with others, it can cause considerable problems. If you always give instructions only in a commanding manner, you encounter considerable resistance from people who are not used to it or who prefer a harmonious form of mutual treatment. But if there is no other way because people are too stubborn to move on even with an inaudible command, you don't get very far in many situations. Those who control both and can use them flexibly as needed will therefore be able to deal with more people and constructively solve a range of problems. In this way, you will automatically become a decision-maker rather than others who have limited behavioral variability.

6.3.6 Unhappy, sick people are not broken – they use what they know and have, but in a way that doesn't satisfactorily meet their needs

Those who live in harmony with themselves, accept themselves, their needs and weaknesses with understanding, are satisfied and happy. Whoever tries to be someone else and rejects himself or parts of his personality lives against himself and wastes the strength and time in a senseless struggle against his identity. It gives rise to an unhappy feeling about life and illness. For example, those who try to make a career in a profession that does not suit them are only wasting their skills. Instead, he could find a job more suitable and achieve greater credit and success, and he could have been far more useful to the world.

6.3.7 Everyone acts as best they can at the given moment

Surely you know this from your own experience, you learn something important, and you think: If I had known then, I would not have made that mistake. It is undoubtedly true. But you have had to gather experiences up to this point and integrate them into your personality in order to be able to learn this thing at this very moment. It wasn't possible then, so you did something with a less satisfactory result than you would have done today. In a few years, you will think similarly to something you are doing today. We are all constantly changing, learning, and becoming more competent. Allow yourself to accept your skills today, use them, and be happy that you will know this thing much better tomorrow because you have decided to constant learning and improvement in your life.

6.3.8 Every behavior is valuable and useful in some context

Imagine always being vague, rarely standing by what you say, preferring to criticize others for their mistakes, and avoiding doing anything or taking responsibility for yourself. That would be terrible – you are probably thinking. Who would want to have anything to do with me? I could forget about my job. No one would take me seriously! This behavior would probably not be very beneficial in your environment. But if you were a politician, you would have good prospects for a miraculous rise. This example may seem a bit exaggerated, but think about it: there are so many different life situations, cultures, and subcultures. It doesn't matter what you do: in at least one context of life, it would make sense for you to do so.

6.3.9 The more options a person can use to shape his life, the smoother and more satisfying his life will be

A high degree of adaptability allowed a man to survive and also to establish himself in extreme environmental conditions. Those who are not flexible destroy themselves in ever-changing life situations. The only permanent thing in life is a change. Therefore, NLP helps to create more options than dealing with problem-solving.

6.3.10 Everyone is capable of achieving everything – in their own way

Anyone who tries to do things the way someone else does will achieve less than the original one and will need more effort and time to do it. But whoever uniquely goes towards the goal will achieve a unique result.

6.3.11 Everyone has everything they need to handle life's problems – they just have to learn how to use it appropriately

Neurolinguistic programming teaches these methods.

6.3.12 There is no such a thing as failure, only results

When you find yourself repeatedly achieving results that do not bring success or credit in the present, think about whether other life situations require such results. It depends on the context whether the result of an action is considered a success or a failure.

6.3.13 Problems taste better in smaller doses

By taking sufficiently small steps, every issue can be solved. How do you eat an elephant? – Little by little.

6.3.14 Behind every problematic behavior is a good intention

NLP is based on the fact that every, even the most meaningless behavior, is at a given time, from the perspective of a part of the subconscious, the most meaningful thing that an individual can do to manage his life in the short term.

6.4 Pillars of NLP in practice

In every company, some employees are more capable of above-average performance than the rest of them. Their success can be achieved by modeling. Top performances are researched, broken down to the smallest detail, and reproduced. For example, with top athletes, where modeling is common, there are slight differences mainly in the mental area, i.e., in the way athletes mentally control their behavior. In modeling, the mental patterns of the model (in this case, a successful manager) are decoded. Not only cognitive strategies (mental processes) are examined, but also motivational elements of actions. In addition, the environment is also taken into account, which sometimes significantly affects the extraordinary performance of a person (Tomašovič, 2015).

According to the author, modeling has the following phases:

- *Setting the goal.* The purpose, what do we want to achieve through modeling? The answer to this question depends on who will be the role model for either the manager or other employees (we imitate only those qualities that are essential for success).
- *Choosing who will serve as a role model.* It is good if more role models are available: by comparing several successful people, essential qualities are revealed more quickly.
- *Determining the components of behavior and attitude that will be the subject of modeling.* Responsible basics for the significant difference from the rest of the average environment.
- *Observing the selected model.* The modeler observes selected excellent candidates in the activities they want to model, for example, a real estate agent selling a house. He notices visible behavior and tries to determine what mental processes are running, and what is happening in the head and body. Then he checks observations and conclusions on simulated cases by asking him to repeat certain activities or by following up again.
- *Comparison.* Comparing an excellent worker with other reference persons and trying to reveal the strategies responsible for extraordinary success. This knowledge is summarized in a model, and tests determine whether a comparable result can be achieved by using the same or similar procedures. The compiled model describes how something works, so its measure is functionality. The theoretical justification of why the model reflects reality is of little importance.

This phase is followed by managerial learning and training. Based on it, skills and attitudes are trained, which are responsible for above-average performances.

It is reasonable to first recruit managers who already show certain characteristics similar to the selected model used in the training sessions. For them, only some properties need to be activated. Transfer into practice is immediate. Acquired skills and attitudes are strengthened if they are combined with intensive individual coaching (Tomašovič, 2015).

According to the author, success factors depend on:

- personality type,
- basic belief,
- strategies,
- mental preparation for events (the opposite of professional training),
- focusing attention on only one thing – focus,
- the ability to control your emotions.

The author summarized the modeling in the following steps:

1. Selection of patterns.
2. Naming the success factors.
3. Concentration of factors into an expert model.
4. Testing the model for reliability and transferability.
5. Training proposal based on the model.
6. Training of trainers to transfer the model.

It often happens that even if a person knows, he does not know how to place it into practice. It is possible that even if we know the basic pillars of NLP, we do not know how to reproduce and apply them in practice.

In the following chapters of a monograph, we present a description and results of analysis of the research carried out in the field of neuromarketing in the context of communication skills, as an essential part of NLP and neurolinguistic programming techniques.

7 Research in the field of neuromarketing, business behavior and NLP

Behavior in general, but also business behavior, can be divided into two forms: prosocial form and undesirable form of behavior. The category of prosocial behavior, such as welcoming behavior in the store, includes the assertive and engaged behavior of business people. The category of undesirable behavior includes manipulative behavior and behavior of traders under the influence of stress. The first presented research focuses on the stated determinants of purchasing behavior from the point of view of customers and from the point of view of merchants.

A theoretical part of the monograph deals with the issue of neurolinguistic programming and neuromarketing. We proceeded to characterize terms related to the field of neuromarketing and neurolinguistic programming, where we also defined determinants of neurolinguistic programming and their possible use. The second research presented focuses on the mentioned concepts in the framework of business behavior.

7.1 Sensory marketing research as an attribute of neuromarketing and business behavior

Behavior in general, but also business behavior, can be divided into two forms: prosocial form and undesirable form of behavior. The category of prosocial behavior, such as welcoming behavior in the store, includes the assertive and engaged behavior of business people. The category of undesirable behavior includes manipulative behavior and behavior of merchants under the influence of stress. The presented research project focuses on mentioned determinants of business behavior from the point of view of customers and traders.

As a part of the first research project of the monograph, SM-CEB, DOBB-T and DOBB-C methodologies were used to conduct the research, with the help of which statistical analysis was performed to clarify research problems.

7.1.1 The aim and hypotheses of the first research project

The goal of the first research project was to enrich knowledge in the field of sensory marketing as an attribute of neuromarketing in terms of identifying associations and differences in the perception and assessment of sensory marketing attributes between traders and customers. The above specification of connections and differences was made in the context of business behavior between traders and customers at a general level. Based on the stated goal, research problems and hypotheses were established:

Problem 1a: Are there statistically significant relationships in the assessment of selected attributes of sensory marketing and determinants of business behavior?
Hypothesis 1a: *We assume that a statistically significant relationship in the assessment of selected attributes of sensory marketing and determinants of business behavior exists.*
Problem 2a: Are there statistically significant differences in the assessment of selected sensory marketing attributes between traders and customers?
Hypotheses 2a: *We assume that statistically significant differences in the assessment of selected attributes of sensory marketing between traders and customers exist.*

7.1.2 Methodologies and methods of the first research project

Empirical research, the most common form of research in the social sciences, was applied to investigate determinants of business behavior. The questionnaire method was used as the main research method. The beginning of the questionnaire contained statements to find out socio-demographic data about the respondents. Statements in the questionnaire were formulated as descriptive, clear, comprehensible, non-suggestive, and without a double negative, so when presenting questionnaires to respondents, there was no mistake in filling them out and the wording of items corresponded with the self-assessment of traders and the perception of customers.

As part of the research, the **SM-CEB methodology** (Sensory Marketing – Cognition, Emotions, Behavior) by Birknerová, Miško, and Ondrijová (2022) was used. It consists of 15 statements focusing on three attributes of sensory marketing:

1. *Cognition*: includes the intensity of thinking, mental processes that serve to process processes and analyze the course of the activity and understand the emotional side, i.e., way of perception, interpretation of certain situations, and perception of oneself and one's abilities, perception of another's behavior, perception of the situation, etc.
2. *Emotions*: feelings of each individual in the external and internal organism influence decision-making, and variability evokes a certain kind of emotion, which can manifest itself differently at each moment. Vysekalová (2011) defines emotions as complex phenomena formed by feelings as ways of experiencing and behaving, accompanied by physiological functions, based on conscious and unconscious evaluation of a subjectively perceived situation.

3. **Behavior**: includes all activities carried out in connection with business conduct, i.e., in connection with purchasing behavior and use of products and services; business behavior goes through the entire decision-making process.

The second questionnaire assessed determinants of business behavior: DOBB–C for customers and DOBB–T for traders (Birknerová, Kovaľová, 2020).

The customer's determinants survey questionnaire consists of two parts. The first part consists of 48 statements divided into four assessed determinants, which were targeted at the perception of selected determinants of the purchasing *behavior of traders from the customer's point of view*. Items 1–12 analyze the manipulative behavior of the trader, items 13–24 the committed behavior and awareness of the trader, items 25–36 the stressed behavior of the trader, and 37–48 analyze the assertive behavior of the trader.

The questionnaire of examination of a trader's determinants was focused on self-assessment within selected determinants of purchasing behavior of traders in relation to customers. It consists of 48 statements divided into four assessed determinants. Items 1–12 analyze *the self-evaluation of the manipulative behavior of a trader*, 13–24 the self-evaluation of the behavior of the trader and *his awareness*, items 25–36 the self-evaluation of *the stressed behavior of a trader*, items 37–48 analyze the self-evaluation of *the assertive behavior of the trader*.

Respondents expressed their opinion using a Likert numerical scale from 1 to 6, where 1 absolutely no, 2 no, 3 no more than yes, 4 yes more than no, 5 yes, 6 definitely yes, in both cases.

The established hypotheses were verified by statistical analysis in the statistical program SPSS 28 using appropriate mathematical and statistical methods. The Kolmogorov-Smirnov test evaluated the data distribution, the result of which indicated a normal distribution of the data, which then enabled the use of the parametric Pearson correlation coefficient.

7.1.3 Research sample of the first research project

The research sample consisted of 167 respondents, of which 86 (51.50 %) were traders, and 81 (48.50 %) were customers. Respondents were separated in terms of gender into 70 (41.92 %) men and 97 (58.08 %) women. 75 (44.91 %) respondents with secondary education and 92 (55.09 %) with university education took part in the research. The average age of the respondents was 29.33 years. There were 46 (53.50 %) men and 40 (46.50 %) women in the group of traders. There were 39 (48.15 %) men and 42 (51.85 %) women in the group of customers. The snowball method was carried out online through Google Docs.

7.1.4 Results of the first research project

In the research, attention was focused on the data distribution analysis as a basic assumption for the use of parametric statistical tests. Based on the results of testing the normality of the data distribution (Table 7.1), it is possible to consider the use of parametric statistics.

Table 7.1. The Kolmogorov-Smirnov test for normality

	Statistic	df	Sig.
Manipulation	0,077	167	0,298
Engagement	0,103	167	0,369
Stress	0,061	167	0,121
Asertivity	0,096	167	0,236
Cognition	0,088	167	0,445
Emotions	0,086	167	0,184
Behavior	0,089	167	0,601

(source: own processing)

Table 7.1 confirms the normal distribution of the data based on a significance level of $p < 0.05$. The Kolmogorov-Smirnov test assumes that the data come from a normal distribution which allows using parametric tests.

Table 7.2 provides an overview of descriptive statistics: means with 95 % confidence intervals, based on which we know that with a probability of 95 %, the entire population would respond in the same way.

Table 7.2. Descriptive statistics and confidence intervals – DOBB

		mean	lower interval	upper interval
Manipulation	trader	3,3711	3,2242	3,5181
	customer	3,9949	3,8834	4,1063
Engagement	trader	4,7975	4,6305	4,9645
	customer	4,0576	3,8668	4,2485
Stress	trader	4,0223	3,8605	4,1841
	customer	4,2860	4,1521	4,4199
Asertivity	trader	4,8953	4,7476	5,0431
	customer	4,6831	4,5264	4,8398

(source: own processing)

Table 7.2 presents the mean values of traders and customers with a 95 % confidence interval. The lowest average score is achieved in the case of manipulation. However, we observe a difference in averages, where traders reported using manipulative behavior less in comparison to customers' ratings. With a 95 % probability, the entire population in the interval 3.883 – 4.106 would give the same opinion. The result that the manipulation reached the lowest score can be attributed to the fact that customers can be subconsciously manipulated in the sense of neuromarketing and manipulation may not even notice.

The fact that traders achieved a lower average score is the problem of the questionnaire method and the problem of subjectivity, so in this case, the opinion of customers is more important. It is also confirmed by Bell et al. (2018) that questionnaire methods are often accompanied by problems of overestimated or underestimated evaluation, distorted responses, and the inability to capture consumers' unconscious reactions.

The highest average score is achieved in assertiveness. Assertive behavior is very important in social interaction and selling itself. For traders, this style of behavior can help to attract customers. Customers want to be respected when buying in terms of honest communication from a trader. With 95 % probability, the entire population in the interval 4.526 – 4.839 would give the same opinion. In the case of engagement, marketers think they are engaged, but from the customer's point of view, it is less, given the average score achieved.

The involvement of a trader is another significant determinant that has an irreplaceable place in the purchasing process. In the case of stress, it is not only the sales process but the overall daily stress level and sensitivity to the stressful situations of the customer. The question is whether it is within the trader's competence to decrease the customer's stress level during the purchase. We hypothesize that unobserved variables such as personality, stress management, and stress sensitivity would help to clarify the stated issue.

Table 7.3 offers an overview of descriptive statistics for SM-CEB methodology with confidence intervals.

Table 7.3. Descriptive statistics and confidence intervals – SM-CEB

	position	mean	lower interval	upper interval
Cognition	trader	4,5953	4,4415	4,7492
	customer	4,0889	3,9047	4,2731
Emotions	trader	4,5395	4,3765	4,7025
	customer	4,3975	4,2231	4,5720
Behavior	trader	4,6977	4,5287	4,8666
	customer	4,0642	3,8648	4,2636

(source: own processing)

The highest average score was achieved in behavior. However, in all cases, we observe that customers scored lower on average than traders. This result is possible since marketers are highly trained, educated, and experienced, and thus more aware of the effects of neuromarketing stimuli in the context of sensory marketing attributes of cognition, emotion, and behavior.

Habib and Qayyum (2018) conducted research in Pakistan on a sample of 317 respondents and focused on similar attributes such as cognitive processing and emotional response of customers in online shopping. They show that customers' emotional responses are particularly important for their purchase decisions, trust in the seller, and thus increase the tendency to make future purchases, even impulsive ones. They also point to the problem that customers' emotional responses are often unconscious, thus complicating their analysis and interpretation. Similar results and problems in the research were observed by Lench (2013), who states that cognition, emotions, and behavior are important aspects of purchase decision, but evolutionary, cultural, technological, and other problems of purchase stereotypes enter here.

Table 7.4. Relationships between selected attributes of sensory marketing and determinants of business behavior – *customers*

SM-CEB / DOBB-C	Cognition	Emotions	Behavior
Manipulation	,279*	-,301**	,378**
	0,037	0,020	0,030
Engagement	0,326	,478**	,302*
	0,677	0,000	0,044
Stress	,299*	-,501**	,399**
	0,446	0,000	0,000
Asertivity	0,299	,533**	0,301
	0,090	0,000	0,090

(source: own processing)
** P ≤ 0.01   * P ≤ 0.05

Table 7.4 presents the answers of customers and relationships of mentioned methodologies. Customers who feel manipulated are more aware of neuromarketing stimuli in the context of sensory marketing of cognitions, emotions, and behaviors. They are more focused on product information and tangible stimuli (cognitions) and adapt their behavior more to the manipulation of the marketer, which eventually can indicate a purchase decision. Conversely, when customers rated the manipulativeness of traders as higher, they experience less positive emotions, similar to stress. In the case of engagement was proven a positive connection with emotions. The more committed customers were to traders, the more positive emotions they experienced during the purchase. However, as we mentioned above, this factor can be determined by other unobserved variables that participate in the level of experiencing stress and coping strategies (gender, education, personality, etc.). The last result shows that customers who evaluated the seller's assertiveness as favorable have more positive emotions from the purchase, similar to engagement.

Ahearne (2021) points to the existing reality where, in addition to following the customer, engaging with him, assertiveness, and choosing the right communication, marketers must focus on the technological transformation, which drastically changes the initial understanding of a trader-customer interaction. Of course, we support the idea that assertiveness and commitment are positive qualities of business people. Atefi (2020) argues that the assumption of an advantage – that sellers have private information about their products and services that buyers do not know – is no longer relevant in many contexts due to buyers' easy access to information before their interaction with a seller. In addition to the information evolution during the COVID-19 pandemic, the online area has become the major format for buyer-seller interaction worldwide (Grewal et al., 2020).

These significant changes only support the idea that there exists a need for continued research in the field of consumer behavior to reflect these changes.

Table 7.5. Relationships between selected attributes of sensory marketing and determinants of business behavior – *traders*

SM-CEB / DOBB-T	Cognition	Emotions	Behavior
Manipulation	-0,065	0,016	-0,121
	0,406	0,841	0,120
Engagement	,601**	,499**	,559**
	0,000	0,000	0,000
Stress	-,535**	-,333*	-,488**
	0,000	0,018	0,000
Asertivity	,596**	,599**	,526**
	0,000	0,000	0,000

(source: own processing)
** P ≤ 0.01   * P ≤ 0.05

Table 7.5 shows the result that marketers' manipulativeness is not related to their personal perception of sensory-marketing stimuli in the context of cognitions, emotions, and behavior. On the contrary, all other results are statistically significant and show a positive association. Traders who think they are more engaged, less stressful, and more assertive with customers are rated as more perceptive of neuromarketing stimuli in the context of customer cognition, emotion, and behavior. In this context, we may interpret it as follow: salespeople who are more focused on product information and material incentives experience positive emotions during sales and adapt behavior accordingly, and try to be more engaged, less stressed, and more assertive in the sales process.

Based on Tables 7.4 and 7.5, we can answer research problem no. 1a that there are relationships between the selected determinants of SM-CEB and DOBB.

We confirm the H1a hypothesis so that there is a statistically significant relationship in the assessment of selected attributes of sensory marketing and determinants of business behavior.

Table 7.6 compares statistically significant differences in the assessment of determinants of sensory marketing of the ZM-KES methodology with consideration of the position, and its results allow to answer to research problem no. 2a.

Table 7.6. Statistically significant differences between traders and customers in terms of Cognition, Emotions, Behavior

	position	mean	t-test	Sig.
Cognition	trader	4,595	3,323	0,000
	customer	4,088		
Emotions	trader	4,539	0,477	0,723
	customer	4,397		
Behavior	trader	4,690	4,409	0,000
	customer	4,064		

(source: own processing)

Table 7.6 presents two statistically significant differences. This result is understandable since we assume that traders are more skilled and have more experience in knowing what is important in the actual purchase. In this context, they, therefore, obtained a higher average score. On the contrary, customers are often not aware of the subconscious processes involved in purchasing decisions. From an ethical point of view, traders should not use this to their advantage, but every trader wants to be successful. It is what neuromarketing research deals with, where marketers want to know the subconscious reactions of customers. In this context, we draw attention to the ethics of neuromarketing research, where research results cannot be used to manipulate and develop sales strategies that are not fair to customers.

Based on the results from Table 7.6, we confirm hypothesis H2a, that there are statistically significant differences in the assessment of selected attributes of sensory marketing between traders and customers.

7.1.5 Summary results of the first research project

Neuromarketing combines the professional discipline of neuroscience with marketing, whose goals and tools are questioned regarding their impact on the individual and society. This is also why neuromarketing is attractive in the media field, while the media's interest in this phenomenon is often not aimed at presenting an objective view. However, neuromarketing does not provide miracle solutions for individual businesses or marketing departments. There are a lot of critical opinions about neuromarketing, especially about the methods it uses, technologies themselves, the correctness of the data obtained, and their relevance in general, their application, interpretation, and repeatability are questioned. Based on the analytical part within the evaluation of the attributes of sensory marketing and business behavior, the monograph focuses on 2 research problems.

Problem 1a: Are there statistically significant relationships in the assessment of selected attributes of sensory marketing and determinants of business behavior? The stated result points to the difference that, in the case of traders, they were assessed as not using manipulative behavior towards customers, so there was no statistically significant association or ZM-KES. On the contrary, customers assessed that they feel more manipulated and then focus more on tangible things during the purchase, experience more negative emotions, and adjust their behavior accordingly. They experience positive emotions with a committed and assertive businessman.

They experience more negative emotions with a stressed trader. Traders who are more focused on product information, and tangible stimuli, experience positive emotions, adapt their behavior accordingly and then try to be more engaged, less stressful, and more assertive in the sales process, i.e., reproduce their own experiences.

Engagement and a strong emotional connection influence customer behavior. Engagement is based on an emotional state. Customers are inclined to help engaged traders, who they see as an added value to the organization. Customers are getting advice when choosing, which is also a motivation for a trader especially when the customer leaves satisfied and with the feeling of a good choice of product. Therefore, it is advisable if a trader uses positive engagement and avoids manipulative behavior.

The manipulative business behavior of traders causes negative emotions in customers. The stressful shopping environment, associated with manipulative elements of trader's business behavior, discomforts customers, often leading them to leave the store. Customers value more the behavior of a trader who is non-violent, honest, attentive, and respectful of the customer's opinion.

Engaged business behavior is manifested as a motivation to buy products faster, as it is also characterized by awareness of the given product that increases the product value for the buyer. This form of trader behavior is highly positively correlated with assertive trading behavior that is respectful, in which the trader is in control of his emotions and communicative, honest, and attentive. It is an appropriate form of behavior in business, as satisfaction motivates traders.

It is appropriate if the businessman is aware of what assertive behavior is, as well as his values, and respects others. If there is no balance between the needs of a trader and a customer, non-assertive behavior occurs. A trader must be able to adopt an assertive attitude by providing constructive feedback. Feedback is important.

Problem 2a: Are there statistically significant differences in the judgment of selected sensory marketing attributes between traders and customers? Within this research problem, test results confirmed statistically significant associations only among traders in determinants of cognition and behavior. This means that traders perceive the customer, his feelings, opinions, and needs in purchasing behavior, i.e., they do not perceive him only as a homogeneous group, but perceive him as the individual in specific situations and adapt accordingly.

How a trader influences a customer's buying behavior results from how he treats and approaches him and communicates with him. A marketer needs to know customers and try to understand their emotional side. Engaged behavior and assertiveness are positive business behaviors. Negative business behavior is manipulative and under the influence of stress.

When it comes to assertive behavior, openness and communication are important in traders, which customers appreciate very quickly. As part of assertive behavior, for businessmen, it is good to know techniques and the phenomena of assertive behavior: being able to praise, accept praise, criticize, accept criticism, requests, rejection of unauthorized requests, etc. An assertive businessman must be self-confident with respect for the rights of others.

Positive behavior leads to the willingness, to help a customer with a choice and decision. The openness and communicativeness of a trader positively affect the purchasing behavior of the customer. The behavior of traders should, therefore, be committed and assertive. Within behavior, customer engagement is a very good strategy. When it is possible to obtain inaccessible data with its help, it is beneficial.

Although opinions in neuromarketing science differ, it still represents a useful tool with relatively large potential, but only on the condition that its attributes and techniques are not misused for customer manipulation or unfair business practices. In addition, we also recall the above opinion of Atefi (2020) that if seller have private information about products and services that buyers do not know about – it is no longer relevant in many contexts, among other things, by changing the communication flow during the COVID-19 pandemic.

7.2 Neuromarketing research and neurolinguistic programming

As a part of the second research project of the monograph, we used SSP, NLP communication, and NLP techniques methodologies to conduct research, with the help of which we performed statistical analysis of specified research problems.

7.2.1 The aim and hypotheses of the second research project

Based on the theoretical study of the associations between neurolinguistic programming and neuromarketing, the analysis of the researched issue, the processing of available sources and professional literature, basic research goals were set:

- to find out and specify the determinants of neurolinguistic programming application (versatility) in the concept of neuromarketing;
- to identify and assess selected neuromarketing attributes.

Considering the research objective of the monograph, the following research problems and hypotheses were determined:

Problem 1b: Are there statistically significant relationships between the assessment of selected NLP-C factors (neuro-linguistic programming – communication) and the assessment of NM-SSP factors (neuromarketing – store, seller, product)?

Hypothesis 1b: *We assume that there are statistically significant relationships between the assessment of selected NLP-C factors and the assessment of NM-SSP factors.*

Indicators: Neurolinguistic programming technique, Neuromarketing store, seller, product.

Problem 2b: Are there statistically significant relationships between the assessment of selected NLP-T factors (neuro-linguistic programming – – techniques) and the assessment of NM-SSP factors (neuromarketing – store, seller, product)?

Hypothesis 2b: *We assume that there are statistically significant associations between the assessment of selected NLP-T factors and the assessment of NM-SSP factors.*

Indicators: Neurolinguistic programming communication, Neuromarketing store, seller, product.

7.2.2 Methodologies and methods of the second research project

In the second research project, we performed quantitative research in which we used methods of empirical data collection, as well as mathematical and statistical methods (Kolmogorov-Smirnov normality test, Descriptive statistics, confidence intervals, Pearson's correlation coefficient) in the IBM SPSS Statistics 26 program. The collection of empirical data was carried out by the questionnaire method and was realized by the snowball method.

Methodologies:

1. *The NLP Technique Questionnaire* was prepared according to the NLP-T methodology and set factors:
   (a) representative systems – questions no. 1 – 5,
   (b) report – questions no. 6 – 10,
   (c) leading – questions no. 11. – 15.

2. *The NLP Communication Questionnaire* was created according to a NLP-C methodology and set factors:
   (a) body language – questions no. 1. – 4,
   (b) active listening – questions no. 5 – 8,
   (c) assertive behavior – questions no. 9 – 12,
   (d) asking questions – questions no. 13. – 17.

3. The *Neuromarketing Questionnaire* was prepared according to the NM-SSP methodology, in which the following factors were set:
   (a) shop,
   (b) seller,
   (c) product.

NLP-C methodology (Neuro-Linguistic Programming – Communication)

It determines the communication skills of individuals and the importance of communication itself. The methodology contains 17 items that are assessed on a 5-point Likert scale. Four factors were extracted by factor analysis. The authors of the methodology describe these factors as follows (Frankovský et al., 2018):

Asking questions – one of the important communication skills is the art of asking the right questions appropriately. The truth is that if we want to get a reasonable answer to a question, we have to ask it correctly. By asking questions, we can obtain, specify and verify information, but also support or block individual communication. For this reason, asking questions must be thought out in advance, but also purposeful, so that the communication does not differ from the chosen topic.

Active listening – in many concepts we meet the requirement to be able to listen to a partner in communication, while the ability to listen to a partner while communicating is not only one of the basic communication skills but also a basic condition for effective communication. Active listening creates an atmosphere of trust and interest in problems, knowledge, and information. Active listening also makes it possible to verify the correctness of the interpretation of the message by the communication partner. On the contrary, reluctance to listen, suppressing listening by talking, interrupting speech, and verbal or non-verbal expressions of interference reduce the effectiveness of communication or disrupt it.

Body language – identifying and interpreting non-verbal communication expressions is an important communication skill. According to many authors, non-verbal communication (body language) includes eye movements, kinesis, gestures, haptics, proxemics, paralinguistics, posturology, facial expressions and others. Body language expresses a person's emotions and inner attitudes, sometimes more than spoken expression. It is the so-called first expression and can reveal a lot to an experienced observer.

Assertiveness – assertiveness is an important part and condition of effective communication. It is based on unpretending (natural) human behavior, while we can adapt it to needs. The goal of assertive communication in the meaning of healthy self-confidence is the authentic expression of emotions, adequate communication of one's attitudes and demands, and staying in one's place. It is about acquiring sufficient communication skills within interpersonal relations while respecting moral principles.

NLP-T methodology (Neuro-Linguistic Programming – Techniques)

This methodology discovers neurolinguistic programming techniques. The methodology contains 15 items that are assessed on a 5-point Likert-type scale. Three factors were defined by factor analysis. The authors of the methodology describe these factors as follows (Frankovský et al., 2018):

Representational systems – the belief that people perceive the world around them primarily through one of the five sensory systems. Each person has his own, so-called preferred sensory system, which he uses most advantageously and in which he feels best. To visualize experiences, we internally use the same neurological ways as a direct experience. The same neurons generate an electrochemical charge that can be measured by an electromyographic reading device. The thought has direct physical effects, and the mind and the body represent one system.

Report – the report program creates an ideal state of communication based on trust and understanding, which managers and executives can use to influence behavior, initiate change, and persuade people. Communication is one of the principles of success and can be defined as creating a spirit of trust and respect between people to create a higher probability of cooperation. Without a relationship, there would only be one-way communication. It takes practice and authenticity, and it means choosing to accept other people's opinions, observations, or motivations. When we do business with another person, either individually or in a group, we always follow or lead someone. Regardless of how much we know about NLP, we either:

- act similarly to another person (in NLP it is called the succession), it is stimulation,
- or act totally different from the other person (called leadership).

Leading – means leading, accompanying, or managing. A manager influences the behavior of another person. The right behavior of another person is achieved by guiding them when they must become agents of change. It provides more control in communication. Adapting and creating harmony with your partner for a certain time should lead to a sufficient relationship, which then should allow you to lead a partner where you want. In this way, we can use different representative systems of the partner. If the partner follows our lead, we have a good level of cooperation. If the partner does not follow our (your) lead, it is necessary to return to harmony to stimulate and continue with the lead.

Changes should be made gradually and not in a way that is too obvious. This technique can be used as a tool to persuade another person to think, feel and act differently. A therapeutic and pedagogical process of any kind is always based on stimulation, behavior, and guidance.

NM-SSP methodology (Neuromarketing – Shop, Seller, Product)

Using this methodology, the authors Birknerová, Miško, and Tomková (2022) tried to find out to what extent the selected attributes affect the psychological processes of buyers in their purchasing behavior of customers. And that aimed at the emotional side of customers. The NM-SSP methodology contains 30 items that are assessed on a 5-point Likert-type scale, allowing to specify 3 attributes related to neuromarketing, namely:

Store – often referred to as a place that a customer visits for the purpose of buying goods, especially at the point of sale, it is possible to reverse the customer's final decision.

Seller – we define him as an employee of the company who has the primary task of serving the customer with the aim of selling goods. As part of neuromarketing, sellers should divert their customers as much as possible from having to calculate something, consider options, or think too deeply.

Product – can be practically anything designed to satisfy consumer needs. Neuromarketing experts found that potential customers can form a strong association between a product and a certain set of images.

In the questionnaire, respondents assessed each statement on a 5-point Likert scale, while the scale was as follows: 0 – definitely not, 1 – no, 2 – rather no than yes, 3 – rather yes than no, 4 – yes, 5 – definitely yes.

7.2.3 Research sample of the second research project

In the presented second research project, data were obtained from a set of 120 respondents (customers), of which 55 (45.83 %) were men and 65 (54.17 %) were women. Within this set, customers of productive age were approached without further definition of conditions. The average age of customers in the research sample was 30.17 years (standard deviation is 8.22 years), ranging from 19 to 60 years. Based on the demographic data and in terms of residence, 70 (58.33 %) customers participated in the research and marked the city as their residence, and 50 (41.67 %) indicated the countryside as their residence. Based on the obtained demographic data in terms of completed education, 48 (40 %)

customers with secondary education and 72 (60 %) with completed university education participated in the research.

7.2.4 Results of the second research project

The obtained data made it possible to carry out several analyzes related to the investigated issue, which were described in the structure of formulated hypotheses.

The normality test is a basic assumption of statistical procedures, including estimation, hypothesis testing, and forecasting, and its results are in Table 7.7.

In terms of interpreting the results, it is necessary to note that respondents or customers may not be familiar with the NLP term but may still have a natural tendency to behave in that way.

Table 7.7. Kolmogorov-Smirnov test for normality

	Statistic	df	p
Body language	0,112	120	0,188
Active listening	0,119	120	0,327
Assertiveness	0,078	120	0,099
Asking questions	0,082	120	0,446
Representational systems	0,101	120	0,345
Report	0,121	120	0,192
Leading	0,100	120	0,504
Store	0,053	120	0,300
Seller	0,053	120	0,200
Product	0,068	120	0,200

(source: own processing)

The results described in Table 7.1 confirm the normal distribution of the data based on a significance level of $p < 0.05$. The Kolmogorov-Smirnov Test tests the null hypothesis, which assumes that the data come from a normal distribution, allowing the use of parametric tests.

Table 7.8 presents descriptive statistics with confidence intervals for the mean. Below the table is the interpretation of the highest and lowest achieved average in the monitored determinants.

Table 7.8. Descriptive statistics and confidence intervals

	Mean	SD.	Lower interval	Upper interval
Body language	3,621	0,080	3,463	3,779
Active listening	3,850	0,078	3,695	4,005
Assertiveness	3,196	0,084	3,330	3,662
Asking questions	3,520	0,072	3,377	3,663
Representational systems	3,087	0,070	2,949	3,225
Report	3,242	0,072	3,698	3,985
Leading	2,603	0,088	2,428	2,778
Store	3,257	0,067	3,425	3,689
Seller	3,167	0,062	3,045	3,288
Product	2,507	0,091	2,326	2,636

(source: own processing)

The highest average score was achieved by customers in the Active listening factor (3.85) with a 95 % probability in the interval 3.695–4.005. The lowest average score was achieved in the Product factor (2.057) in the interval 2.326–2.636. Active listening evaluates the level of the ability to listen in the context of communication, where we consider it a positive result that the highest average score has been achieved from all the factors assessed within the addressed issue and in the social context. On the contrary, the Product evaluation achieved the lowest score. The product was tracked by items, which neuromarketing stimuli encourage the purchase.

This result may not reflect the real behavior of customers, or they may intentionally or unintentionally claim that incentives such as discounts, advertisements, and contests do not encourage them to buy. This is the main goal of neuromarketing research: to verify how actually presented incentives subconsciously influence buyers.

Table 7.9 shows the results of the correlation analysis. We verified the existence of statistically significant associations between the total score of the NM-SSP neuromarketing methodology and NLP-T and NLP-C.

Context of NM-SSP and NLP methodology with 95 % confidence interval for a correlation coefficient

Table 7.9. Relationships of NM-SSP and NLP methodology with 95 % confidence interval for correlation coefficient

		NLP-T	NLP-C
NM-SSP	Pearson Correlation	,350**	,491**
	Sig. (2-tailed)	0,000	0,000
	95 % Upper	0,498	0,616
	95 % Lower	0,183	0,342

(source: own processing)
** P ≤ 0.01   * P ≤ 0.05

Table 7.9 shows associations between the NM-SSP and NLP-T methodology. Although the correlation coefficients are not high, they are still statistically significant. They point to a positive association, which means that the more the customer reacts in life in terms of NLP (techniques and communication), the more important the store, seller, sroduct factors are for him.

The confidence interval of the correlation coefficient is also calculated, and a 95 % probability applies to the entire population in the interval of NLP-T (0.498–0.183) and NLP-C (0.616–0342). It represents the fact that it is really important to estimate the customer's personality in the context of NLP to adjust sales strategies to improve his evaluation of the store, seller, or product.

Table 7.9 is also supported by the results of statistically significant connections between the factors of individual methodologies within the correlation coefficients themselves, which we present in Tables 7.4 and 7.5.

Table 7.10 shows the results of the correlation analysis between the factors of the NM-SSP and NLP-T methodology, and Table 7.11 shows the existence of statistically significant connections between the factors of the NM-SSP and NLP-C methodologies.

Table 7.10. Relationships of factors of the NN-SSP methodology and factors of the NLP-T methodology

		Representational systems	Report	Leading
Store	Pearson Correlation	,281**	,418**	,204*
	Sig. (2-tailed)	0,002	0,000	0,026
Seller	Pearson Correlation	,356**	,448**	,355**
	Sig. (2-tailed)	0,000	0,000	0,000
Product	Pearson Correlation	,280**	,224*	,326**
	Sig. (2-tailed)	0,002	0,014	0,000

(source:own processing)
** P ≤ 0.01   * P ≤ 0.05

We found the existence of statistically significant associations between all factors, namely: the use of NLP techniques in everyday life of customers and the importance of selected neuromarketing assessment factors: store, seller, and product. All the information we receive, whether in ordinary life or business behavior, originates through our senses (visual, auditory, movement, taste, and smell). The more customers behave in their everyday life in the context of NLP, the more important their perception of neuromarketing tools is. Customers who tend to listen carefully and notice another person, care about trust and emotions in the conversation, pay more attention to the store as a whole, and especially to its cleanliness. They also pay more attention to the seller's mood and the product itself, where the lowest correlation has been verified.

Based on the mentioned results, it is possible to consider hypothesis no. 1b We assume that there are statistically significant relationships between the assessment of selected NLP-T factors and the assessment of NM-SSP factors as verified.

Table 7.11. Relationships of factors of NN-SSP and NLP-T methodologies

		Body language	Active listening	Assertiveness	Asking questions
Store	Pearson Correlation	,230*	,396**	,342**	,209*
	Sig. (2-tailed)	0,011	0,000	0,000	0,022
Seller	Pearson Correlation	,352**	,416**	,442**	,436**
	Sig. (2-tailed)	0,000	0,000	0,000	0,000
Product	Pearson Correlation	0,027	0,066	0,173	0,019
	Sig. (2-tailed)	0,768	0,471	0,098	0,839

(source: own processing)
** P ≤ 0.01   * P ≤ 0.05

The results of the correlation analysis confirmed several statistically significant correlation coefficients. Statistically significant associations were manifested primarily between NLP-C attributes and two NM-SSP instruments (store, salesperson). All correlation coefficients were positive. The higher the customers scored in one indicator, the higher they also scored in the other.

The more customers pay attention to body language, active listening, assertiveness, and asking questions, the more they notice the store as a whole, its cleanliness, and also the salesperson, his mood, and expression.

Based on the mentioned results, it is possible to consider hypothesis no. 2b *We assume that there are statistically significant connections between the assessment of selected NLP-C factors and the assessment of NM-SSP factors as verified.*

Table 7.12 describes the results of the descriptive statistics of methodology of NM-SSP factors with a confidence interval for the mean.

Table 7.12. Descriptive statistics of selected items of the NM-SSP methodology with a 95 % confidence interval

	Mean	SD	Lower interval	Upper interval
Store				
The cleanliness of the store is important to me when shopping.	4,310	0,977	4,130	4,480
Seller				
The range of the assortment offered by seller is important to me.	4,260	0,983	4,080	4,440
The seller's mood affects my purchasing decision.	4,170	0,960	3,980	4,360
The seller's speech influences my purchasing decision.	4,070	0,100	3,870	4,270
Product				
Visual display of the product in a visible place encourages me to buy it.	3,390	0,126	3,140	3,640

(source: own processing)

We have confirmed that for customers who behave and react in terms of NLP are neuromarketing factors more important. Table 7.12 describes the importance of specific items of the SSP methodology. The highest average score was achieved in the Store factor, in the specific item of Cleanliness of the store (4.310). Items with an average score above 4.0 are selected, except for the Product factor, where even the highest-scoring item reached an average below 4.0.

Based on the result, the cleanliness of the store is extremely important for customers, and we can assume that the same result applies to the entire population with a 95 % probability in the interval 4.130–4.480. This is a relatively narrow confidence interval, the lower limit of which is more than 4.0, which represents a 'yes' response on a 5-point Likert scale (0 – definitely not to 5 – definitely yes).

In the Seller factor, an average score was achieved, above 4.0, in three items, namely: The range of the offered assortment, Seller's Mood, and Seller's Speech.

The range of the offered assortment (4.260) and its importance for the entire population are in the interval 4.080 – 4.440. Similarly, the lower limit of the interval is above 4.0.

The Product factor is evaluated in terms of its content page, whether it encourages customers to buy, for example, a discount, competition, and others. It probably caused the mentioned factor not to reach the lower limit of 4.0 because customers do not find the mentioned marketing incentives as encouraging to purchase. As mentioned above, the answers may not reflect reality. It is the goal of neuromarketing research: to verify how presented stimuli subconsciously influence buyers. The highest achieved average score is in the item: Visual display of the product in a visible place (3.390). With 95 % probability, this answer would be selected by the entire population in the interval 3.140–3.640.

7.2.5 Summary results of the second research project

As part of communication, we analyzed selected factors: body language, active listening, assertive behavior, and asking questions. Furthermore, within the framework of techniques, we assessed selected factors: representational systems, report, and leading. From the field of neuromarketing, we evaluated the store, seller, and product factors.

As part of the assessment of the connection between the factors of the NLP-C, NLP-T, and NM-SSP methodologies, we found the existence of statistically significant relationships. From the point of view of the Store factor, it is convenient, when entering the store, to visually see that it is organized and clean. The Store and Product factors influence customers and create associations through the lighting of the offered goods (the intensity and color of the lighting). Marketers learned to use this phenomenon and started to illuminate targeted products with different colors and light intensities to support the customer's decision-making and purchasing behavior. It is, for example, lighting the meat in orange, which visually associates and highlights freshness. Similarly, fruits and vegetables are illuminated in yellow, which supports the visual freshness of the goods. Under neutral lighting, however, the goods may lose their fresh colors and consequently look less attractive. Accordingly, the customer should always look at the product in normal light. The range of the offered goods, the seller's mood, and the expression play an important role in the Seller factor.

Therefore, sales success lies in the identification of a specific customer and the strategy of the seller, which must connect with the customer as much as possible. In the context of NLP, it is therefore important that a trader knows the mentioned techniques and communication style, which will help him to discover the type of customer and adapt to him in terms of NLP. Our results confirm that it is important because it is related to the evaluation of neuromarketing factors: store, seller, and product.

We can assume that NLP techniques work better if customers implement NLP on a conscious or unconscious level. A salesperson who knows techniques and communication styles in the sense of NLP can consequently more easily cooperate with a customer. It will ultimately lead to higher success in terms of sales and customer satisfaction. Similar results provide by Karpová et al. (2019), who emphasize the need for continuous training of salespeople in the framework of NLP, which increases customer loyalty. Arthmann and Li (2017) emphasize that NLP techniques have an important place in the context of neuromarketing. They also state that representational systems are meaningful in the creation of marketing strategies.

It is necessary to understand how a person processes signals. Udo-Imeh (2022) states that personality plays a significant role in consumer buying behavior because consumers differ and have different personality traits that reflect their buying behavior. A serious problem that marketers have to deal with is determining when personality is a significant factor in purchasing decisions and when it is not and how to analyze different personality traits. Chukwu et al. (2020), Gohary (2014), and others have the same opinion on the issue.

The results of the second research project carried out show that customers who consciously or unconsciously use NLP techniques in their everyday life find neuromarketing factors more important.

Results based on questionnaires have limited validity because they may not reflect actual customer preferences, or the results may be significantly skewed. The goal of neuromarketing research is to find out what customers experience and what influences them when making purchasing decisions.

Conclusion

Nowadays, a popular topic that may be seen from numerous perspectives is the neuropsychology of consumer behavior. Regardless of whether we refer to this topic as neuromarketing or the neuroscience of consumer behavior, it is a field that encompasses multiple scientific branches.

The major objective of the monograph was to clarify specific neuromarketing attributes and neurolinguistic programming in business behavior and to compare how businesspeople and customers subjectively perceived these attributes in relation to business behavior. The monograph's other goals included identifying the factors that influence how people behave in the workplace as well as how neurolinguistic programming and sensory marketing fit into the field of neuromarketing.

Using neuromarketing, marketers try to influence customer behavior, either positively or negatively. They are looking for new ways to handle customer decision-making in their favor without the customer even realizing it. As part of fulfilling the goal of the monograph, we state that it was fulfilled.

The research part aimed to identify the factors that influence how neurolinguistic programming is applied to the concept of neuromarketing and to evaluate a few key neuromarketing attributes. In terms of the findings, the monograph's research goal was achieved. We also discussed potential neuromarketing tools that, through the use of NLP, brand enhancement, quality-related suggestions, reputation-building in the market, and brand enhancement, could influence marketers to behave more ethically in their business affairs.

In the research project, we analyzed the existence of statistically significant associations between communication skills, neuro-linguistic programming techniques, and selected attributes of neuromarketing in a questionnaire form. As part of the summary of the research results, we presented how to modify the use of neurolinguistic programming determinants in communication, NLP and neuromarketing techniques in practice and what techniques could be used to achieve success.

Neuromarketing is a scientific discipline that employs neuroscientific tools to examine and comprehend consumer and trader behavior in the context of business. While each of the elements that make up neuromarketing is different and appropriate for different goals, it is undeniable that their combination produces the most trustworthy outcomes. In the continuing trend of differentiating scientific and practical approaches, we see the future of the research of neuromarketing and neurolinguistic programming.

Neuromarketing and marketers use the psychology of creating questions and techniques to gain massive customer influence. First of all, marketers must create a communication strategy adapted to the partner's requirements or customer's needs. With this strategy, they will succeed in achieving a positive response. Furthermore, they must have all their senses on alert and perceive customers' needs. Perceptiveness as part of communication with others is important. When communicating with others, it is significant to adjust to the person with whom they are communicating, respect the other's feelings, and understand the other person based on respect and trust. Neuroscience will deal with a deeper and more detailed investigation of psychological processes to create a theoretical neuropsychological model that will complete traditional psychological, marketing, and economic theories. Practical neuromarketing will focus on testing products and services and their marketing strategies. It will lead to a significant transformation in the entire branch.

Neurolinguistic programming can be described as the key to the success of every businessman or the art of personal success. No concrete definition of neurolinguistic programming was found. It is already clear that the application of NLP to sciences such as marketing and management was inevitable.

The determinants of neurolinguistic programming commonly incorporate psychological techniques. As a result, NLP supports people in understanding both themselves and those around them, enabling them to realize their own aspirations. To succeed, we must be capable of expressing our aims clearly. The brain can be programmed to look for chances to help us reach our goals in this specific situation.

We find the advantages and benefits neurolinguistic programming brings in both private and working life. Based on the theoretical knowledge from the professional literature in the monograph, we think that NLP acts as a flexible tool that is able to adapt to different types of personalities.

We believe that the goals we have established can be accomplished with the help of NLP and the use of communication skills and techniques, but we also realize that NLP does not have an ideal methodology or an abundance of relevant data. In the end, whether a company is large or small, everyone's ability to succeed depends on their ability to communicate and improve their communication skills.

Because all fundamental inputs, including those that are visual, auditory, kinetic, tasteful, and olfactory, emerge from the senses, we believe it is crucial to leverage human potential in both daily activities and commercial practices.

It implies that the importance of neuromarketing techniques will increase as marketers pay more attention to the representational system technique.

It was not possible to examine all the determinants of neuromarketing in further detail due to the monograph's constrained scope. Given that this subject is not accurately and thoroughly addressed in Slovak literature, the monograph attempted to draw on the most accessible corpus of professional literature, particularly international.

References

AČRA-MK. (nedat). Etický kodex. [online]. [cit. 2021-11-13]. Dostupné z: http://www.acra-mk.cz/eticky-kodex/

AGRAWAL, A. 2016. How nlp can boost your marketing influence [online]. 2016, [cit. 2021-11-14]. Dostupné na internete: https://www.forbes.com/sites/ajagrawal/2016/06/12/how-nlp-can-boost-your-marketing-influence/#1dced9887c13>.

AHEARNE, M., ATEFI, Y., LAM, S. K., POURMASOUDI, M. 2021. The future of buyer-seller interactions: A conceptual framework and research agenda. Journal of the Academy of Marketing Science, 50(1), 1–24.

ALEXY, J. 2011. Manažment znalostí a organizačné správanie. Bratislava: Ekonóm. ISBN 978-80-225-3194-8.

ANDREJKOVIČ, M. 2007. Psychológia trhu. Prešov: Metodicko- pedagogické centrum v Prešove. ISBN 978-80-8045-462-3.

ARENI, C. S., KIM, D., 1993. The influence of background music on shopping behavior: Classical versus top-forty music in a wine store. Advances in Consumer Research, 20(1), 336–340.

ARGO, J. J., DAHL, D. W., MORALES, A. C. 2006. Consumer contamination: How consumers react to products touched by others. Journal of Marketing, 70, 81–94.

ARIELY, D., BERNS, G. S. 2010. Neuromarketing: the hope and hype of neuroimaging in business. Nature Reviews Neuroscience, 11(4), 284–292.

ARMSTRONG, M. 1999. Personální management. Praha: Grada Publishing. ISBN 978-80-716-9614-87.

ARTHMANN, C., & LI, I.-P. 2017. Neuromarketing-The Art and Science of Marketing and Neurosciences Enabled by IoT Technologies. *IIC Journal of Innovation*, 1–10.

ATEFI, Y., AHEARNE, M., HOHENBERG, S., HALL, Z., ZETTELMEYER, F. 2020. Open negotiation: The back-end benefits of salespeople's transparency in the front end. JMR, Journal of Marketing Research, 57(6), 1076–1094.

AYDINOĞLU, N. Z., SAYIN, E. 2016. Sensory and neuromarketing: About and beyond customer sensation. In Flavor (pp. 97–408). Woodhead Publishing.

BALL, D. L. 1988. Unlearning to teach mathematics. For the Learning of Mathematics, 8(1), 40–48.

BARNETT, S.B., CERF, M. 2017. A Ticket for Your Thoughts: Method for Predicting Content Recall and Sales Using Neural Similarity of Moviegoers.

Journal of Consumer Research, 44. Published by Oxford University Press on behalf of Journal of Consumer Research.

BARTÁKOVÁ, P. G., GUBÍNIOVÁ, K. 2015. Udržateľný marketingový manažment. Trnava: Inštitút aplikovaného manažmentu. ISBN 978-80-89600-24-3.

BÁRTA, V., PÁTÍK, L., POSTLER, M. 2009. Retail Marketing. 1. vyd. Praha: Management Press. ISBN 978-80-7261-207-9.

BECHARA, A., DAMASIO, H., DAMASIO, A. R. 2000. Emotion, decision making and the orbitofrontal cortex. Cerebral cortex, 10(3), 295–307

BEDRNOVÁ, E., I. NOVÝ a kol. 1998. Psychologie a sociologie řízení. Praha: Manage-ment Press. ISBN 80-85943-57-3.

BELL, L. L. 2016. Neuro-linguistic Programming In the Classroom: The Disney Strategy. Elementary Teacher's Federation of Ontario (ETFO), pp. 30–45.

BELL, L., VOGT, J., WILLEMSE, C., ROUTLEDGE, T., BUTLER, L. T., SAKAKI, M. 2018. Beyond self-report: A review of physiological and neuroscientific methods to investigate consumer behavior. Frontiers in Psychology, 9, 1655

BĚLOHLÁVKOVÁ, V. 2009. Rukověť začínajícího prodejce. Jak se stát dobrým obchodníkem. Praha: Grada Publishing. ISBN 978-80-247-2344-0.

BENNETT, P. O. 1995. Dictionary of marketing terms. Chicago: American Marketing Association. [online]. [cit. 2021-10-23]. Dostupné z: www.marketi ngpower.org/dictionary_aspx.

BERCEA, M. D. 2011. Anatomy of methodologies for measuring consumer behavior in neuromarketing research. [online]. [cit. 2021-11-13]. Dostupné z: https://www.researchgate.net/publication/260058154_Anatomy_of_ methodologies_for_measuring_consumer_behavior_in_neuromarketing_ research.

BERCEA, M. D. 2013. Quantitative versus qualitative in neuromarketing research. MPRA Paper No. 44134. Munich Personal RePEc Archive.

BERČÍK, J., HORSKÁ E., PALUCHOVÁ, J., NEOMÁNIOVÁ, K. 2014. Using of eye tracker in horeca segment: Visual proposal of chosen communication tool on restaurant guests decision. In Euroean journal of bussines science and technology. [online]. [cit. 2021-11-13]. Dostupné z: <file:///H:/28-Submission%20Text%20(Anonymous)%20-%20MS%20 Word%20or%20TeX_LaTeX-128-1-10-20160106.pdf>. ISSN 2336-6494.

BHATIA, T. K. 2000. Advertising in rural India: Language, marketing communication, and consumerism. Tokyo, Japan: Tokyo Press.

BIRKNEROVÁ, Z., FRANKOVSKÝ, M., ZBIHLEJOVÁ, L. 2013. Differences in the perception of machiavellian manifestations between male and female managers. In Journal of Management and Business: Research and Practice. Prešov: FM PU. ISSN 1338-0494.

BIRKNEROVÁ, Z., KOVAĽOVÁ, J. 2020. DOS – Determinanty obchodného správania. Dotazník identifikácie determinantov obchodného správania. Prešov: Bookman, 23 s. ISBN 978-80-8165-391-9.

BIRKNEROVÁ, Z., MIŠKO, D., ONDRIJOVÁ, I. 2022. Zmyslový marketing ako atribút neuromarketingu v kontexte obchodného správania. Prešov: Vydavateľstvo Prešovskej univerzity, 131 s.

BIRKNEROVÁ, Z., MIŠKO, D., TOMKOVÁ, A. 2022. Výskum neuromarketingu v koncepcii s neurolingvistickým programovaním. Prešov: Vydavateľstvo Prešovskej univerzity, 121 s.

BIRKNEROVÁ, Z., TOMKOVÁ, A., ČIGARSKÁ, B. N. 2020. Manifestations of Machiavellianism: assessment of manifestations of manipulation in business behavior. Saarbrucken: Lambert Academic Publishing. 85 p. ISBN 978-620-2-79946-1.

BITNER, M. J., 1992. Servicescapes: The impact of physical surroundings on customers and employees. J. Mark, 56(2), 57–71.

BOČEK, M., JESENSKÝ, D., KROFIÁNOVÁ, D. 2009. POP – In-store komunikace v praxi: trendy a nástroje arketing v místě prodeje. 1. vyd. Praha: Grada Publishing. ISBN 978-80-247-2840-7.

BORGO, A. J. 2006. Neurolinguistické programovanie: Mirage pre vedúcich pracovníkov. Skeptické oko, [online]. 2006, [cit. 2021-10-04]. Dostupné na internete: //www.elojoesceptico.com.ar/revistas/eoe06/eoe0605

BOSMANS, A. 2006. Scents and sensibility: When do (in)congruent ambient scents influence product evaluations? Journal of Marketing, 70(3), 32–43.

BPS. 2022. *Further reading about the Division of Coaching Psychology. History of the Division of Coaching Psychology.* [online]. [cit. 2022-10-04]. Dostupné na internete https://www.bps.org.uk/member-networks/division-coaching-psychology

BRAEUTIGAM, S., STINS, J. F., ROSE, S. P., SWITHENBY, S. J., AMBLER, T. 2001. Magnetoencephalographic signals identify stages in real-life decision processes. Neural Plasticity, 8(4), 241–254.

BRAKUS, J. J., SCHMITT, B. H., ZARANTONELLO, L. 2009. Brand experience: what is it? How is it measured? Does it affect loyalty?. Journal of marketing, 73(3), 52–68.

BRAKUS, J. J., SCHMITT, B. H., ZHANG, S. 2008. Experiential attributes and consumer judgments. In B. H. Schmitt, & D. Rogers (Eds.), Handbook on brand, experience management. Northampton, MA: Edward Elgar.

BRAMMER, M. 2004. Brain scam?. Nature Neuroscience, 7(10), 1015-1015.
BRIERS, S. 2012. Vybuchne mýty generácie vlastnej pomoci. Pearson.
CAHILL, L., BABINSKY, R., MARKOWITSCH, H. J., MCGAUGH, J. L., 1995. The amygdale and emotional memory. Nature, 377(6547), 295-296.
CAPODAGLI, B., JACKSON, L. 1998. The disney way: Harnessing the management secrets of disney in your company. United States of America: Center for Quality Leadership, 1998. 244 s. [online]. [cit. 2021-11-14]. Dostupné na internete: <http://www.scribd.com/doc/3123654/The-Disney-Way>. ISBN 0-07-012064-1.
CHANDON, P., ORDABAYEVA, N. 2009. Downsize in 3D, supersize in 1D: Effects of dimensionality of package and portion size changes on size estimations, consumption, and quantity discount expectations. Journal of Marketing Research, 46(6), 725-738.
CHEBAT, J. C., GELINAS-CHEBAT, C., FILIATRAULT, P. 1993. Interactive effects of musical and visual cues on time perception: An application to waiting lines in banks. Percept. Mot. Skills 77, 995-1020.
COURBET, D., BENOIT, D. 2013. Neurosciences au service de la communication commerciale: manipulation et éthique. Une critique du neuromarketing. Études de communication, (1), 27-42.
CRUSCO, A. H., WETZEL, C. G. 1984. The Midas touch: The effects of interpersonal touch on restaurant tipping. Personality and Social Psychology Bulletin, 10, 512-517.DANI, V., PABALKAR, V. 2013. Branding through sensory marketing. International Journal of Scientific Research, 2(11). ISSN 2277-8179.
DANNHOFEROVÁ, J. 2012. Velká kniha barev: Kompletní průvodce pro grafiky, fotografy a designéry. Brno: Computer Press, Albatros Media a. s. ISBN 978-80-251-3785-7
DAPKEVICIUS, A., MELNIKAS, B. 2009. Influence of price and quality to customer satisfaction: neuromarketing approach. Business in XXI Century, 1(3), ISSN 2029-2252.
DAS, A. 2009. NeuroMarketing – "See" what the consumer thinks [online]. IIM Indore Management Canvas Dostupné na internete: [online]. [cit. 2021-01-24]. Dostupné na internete. <http://www.managementcanvas.iimindore.in/icanvas/index.php?option=com_content&view=article&id=107:neuromarketing-qseeq-what-the-consumer-thinks&catid=34:marketing-and-branding&Itemid=56
DAVIDSON, R. J. 2004. What does the prefrontal cortex "do" in affect: Perspectives on frontal EEG asymmetry research. Biological Psychology, 67(1), 219-234.

DE BONO, E. 1992a. Six thinking hats for schools: Resource book 1. Melbourne, VIC: Hawker Brownlow Education.

DE BONO, E. 1992b. Six thinking hats for schools: Resource book 2. Melbourne, VIC: Hawker Brownlow Education.

DE BONO, E. 1992c. Six thinking hats for schools: Resource book 3. Melbourne, VIC: Hawker Brownlow Education.

DE BONO, E. 2017. Six thinking hats. Penguin UK.

DELWICHE, J. 2004. The impact of perceptual interactions on perceived flavor. Food Quality and Preference, 15(2), 137–146.

DENNISON, L., MOSS-MORRIS, R., & CHALDER, T. (2009). A review of psychological correlates of adjustment in patients with multiple sclerosis. *Clinical Psychology Review, 29*, 141-153.

DENTON, J. 2018. ICC Advertising and marketing communications code. Building consumer trust through responsible marketing [online]. Paríž: Avenue du Président, 2018. 54 s. [cit. 2021-10-10]. Dostupné na internete: <https://cms.iccwbo.org/content/uploads/sites/3/2018/09/icc-advertising-and-marketing-communications-code-int.pdf>. ISBN: 978-92-842-0528-8.

DEVARU, S. D. B. 2018. Significance of neuromarketing on consumer buying behaviour. International Journal of Technical Research & Science Significance, 3, 114–121.

DILTS, R. 1994. Strategies of genius, vol. 1. In Cupertino. California: Metapublications.

DILTS, R. 1996. Visionary leadership skills: Creating a world to which people want to belong, meta. Capitola, CA.

DILTS, R. 1998. Modeling with NLP. USA: Meta Publications. ISBN 9780916990411.

DILTS, R. B. 2008. Strategiide geniu. Vol. I. Bucuresti: Ed. Excalibur.

DILTS, R. B. 2014. Bazele Programarii neuro-lingvistice. Bucuresti: Ed. Vidia.

DILTS, R. B., LOZIER, J. D. 2000. Encyclopedia of systemic NLP and NLP new coding. Scotts Valley: NLP University Press.

DIMBERG, U., LUNDQUIST, L. O. 1990. Gender differences in facial reactions to facial expressions. Biological Psychology, 30(2), 151–159.

DORČÁK, P., POLLÁK, F. 2010. Marketing and e-Business: Ako sa zorientovať v pojmoch a procesoch nového marketingu. Prešov: EZO.sk. 114 s. ISBN 978-80-970564-0-7

DROULERS, O., ROULLET, B. 2007. Émergence du neuromarketing: apports et perspectives pour les praticiens et les chercheurs. In. Décisions Marketing, 2007, č. 46, s. 9–23. ISSN 1253-0476.

DUBOSE, C. N., CARDELLO, A. V., MALLER, O. 1980. Effects of colorants and flavorants on identification, perceived flavor intensity, and hedonic quality of fruit-flavored beverages and cake. Journal of Food Science, 45(5), 1393–1399.

DUDINSKÁ, E. a kol. 2000. Základy marketingu. Bratislava: Ekonóm, 2000. 199 s. ISBN 80-225-1222-2.

DUDINSKÁ, E., ŠTEFKO, R. a kol. 2006. Základy marketingu. Bratislava: Ekonóm. 193 s. ISBN 80-225-1222-2

EICHENBAUM, H. 1996. Olfactory perception and memory. In R. R. Llinas, & R. Smith Churchland (Eds.), The mind-brain continuum (pp. 173–202). Cambridge, MA: MIT Press.

ELANGOVAN, N., PADMA, C. 2017. Neuro marketing: The new marketing paradigm. International Journal of Business and Management Invention, 6(3), 30–34.

FARLEY A. 2020. Positive mental qualities of successful traders [online]. [cit. 2021-10-27]. Dostupné z: https://www.investopedia.com/ articles/professionals/062215/characteristics-successful-traders.asp

FAVIER, M., CELHAY, F., PANTIN-SOHIER, G. 2019. Is less more or a bore? Package design simplicity and brand perception: An application to Champagne. Journal of Retailing and Consumer Services, 46, 11–20

FERREL, O., HARTLINE, M. 2010. Marketing Strategy. Mason, USA: Cengage Learning. s. ISBN 0-538-46738-X

FISCHER, C., CHIN, L., KLITZMAN, R. 2010. Practices and professional challenges. Harvard Review of Psychiatry, 18(4), 230–237.

FOSCHT, T., SWOBODA, B. 2004. Käuferverhalten Grundlagen — Perspektiven — Anwendungen. Journal für Marketing 43, 166. https://doi.org/10.1007/BF03032248

FOSCHT, T., SWOBODA, B. 2011. Käuferverhalten: Grundlagen, Perspektiven, Anwendungen. 4 th Edition. Wiesbaden: Gabler.

FRANKOVSKÝ, M. a kol. 2018. Digital communication management. London: IntechOpen. ISBN 978-1-78923-514-2.

FURDUESCU, B. A. 2019. NLP methods of motivation: Metaprograms and reframing. Holistica, 10(1), 127–138.

GIBSON, B. 2011. The complete guide to understanding and using NLP: Neuro-linguistic programming explained simply. Florida: Atlantic Publishing Company. ISBN 978-1-60138-382-2.

GOHARY, A., HANZAEE, K. H. 2014. Personality traits as predictors of shopping motivations and behaviors: A canonical correlation analysis. Arab Economic and Business Journal, 9(2), 166–174.

GRAHAM, J. R., HARVEY, C. R., HUANG, H. 2009. Investor competence, trading frequency, and home bias. Management Science, 55, 1094 – 1106. ISSN 0025-1909.

GRAY, R. M., LIOTTA, R. F. 2012. PTSD: Extinction, reconsolidation and the visual kinesthetic dissociation protocol. Traumatology, 18(2), 3–16

GREWAL, D., HULLAND, J., KOPALLE, P. K., KARAHANNA, E. 2020. The future of technology and marketing: A multidisciplinary perspective. Journal of the Academy of Marketing Science, 48(1), 1–8.

GRIMLEY, B. 2013. Theory and practice of NLP coaching: A psychological approach, Sage, London.

GRIMLEY, B. 2016. What is NLP? The development of a grounded theory of NeuroLinguistic Programming, (NLP), within an action research journey. International Coaching Psychology Review, 11(2), 166–178.

GRUNWALD, M. 2008. Human haptic perception: Basic and applications. Basel: Birkhäuser Verlag. ISBN 978-3-7643-7611-6.

HABIB, D., M., QAYYUM, A. 2018. Cognitive emotion theory and emotion-action tendency in online impulsive buying behavior. Journal of Management Sciences, 5(1), 86–99.

HAECKEL, S. H., CARBONE, L. P., BERRY, L. L. 2003. How to lead the customer experience. Marketing Management, 12(1), 18–23.

HALL, M. 2001. *The Structure of Personality (Nlp and Neuro-Semantics Approach)*. Crown House Publishing Ltd. ISBN-10 1899836675.

HAMDY, A., ELHOSEINY, M. a kol. 2009. Mind maps automation system. Proceeding of the 2009 International Conference on Semantic Web & Web Services, SWWS 2009, At Las Vegas, Nevada, USA.

HERMAN, P. C., POLIVY, J., KLAJNER, F., ESSES, V. M. 1981. Salivation in dieters and non-dieters. Appetite 2 (4), 356–361.

HERZ, R. S. 2004. A naturalistic analysis of autobiographical memories triggered by olfactory visual and auditory stimuli. Chemical Senses, 29(3), 217–224.

HERZ, R. 2007. The scent of desire: Discovering our enigmatic sense of smell. New York, NY: William Morrow.

HERZ, R. S., ENGEN, T. 1996. Odor memory: Review and analysis. Psychonomic Bulletin and Review, 3(3), 300–313.

HLOUŠKOVÁ, J. 2016. Emocionální inteligence jako základní premisa leadershipu. In: HR forum. [online]. [cit. 2021-01-10]. Retrieved from: <http://www.hrforum.cz/emocionalni-inteligence-jako-zakladni-premisa-leadership/>. ISSN 1212-690X.

HOCH, S. J. 2002. Product experience is seductive. Journal of Consumer Research, 29(3), 448–454.

HORÁKOVÁ, I. 1995. Marketing v současné světové praxi. Praha: Grada Publishing. 364 s. ISBN 978-80-854-2483-6.

HOŠKOVÁ, B. 2012. Vademecum. Zdravotní tělesná výchova (druhy oslabení). Praha: Karolinum. ISBN 978-80-246-2137-1.

HUI, M. K., BATESON, E. G. 1991. Perceived control and the effects of crowding and consumerchoice on service experience. Journal of Consumer Research, 18(2), 174–184.

HUI, M. K., DUBE, L., CHEBAT, J. C. 1997. The impact of music on consumers' temporal perceptions: Does time fly when you are having fun? The Journal of Retail, 73, 87–104.

HULTÉN, B. 2011. Sensory marketing: The multi-sensory brand-experience concept. European Business Review, 23(3), 256–273.

HULTÉN, B. 2017. Branding by the five senses: A sensory branding framework. Journal of Brand Strategy, 6(3), 281–292.

HULTÉN, B., BROWEUS, N., DIJK, M. V. 2009. Sensory marketing. London: Pallgrave Macmillan. ISBN 978-1-349-36649-1

HUSZÁR, S., PAP, K. 2016. Revolutionising marketing research? A critical view on the promising neuromarketing. *Value Chains: Regional Clusters, Local Networks and Entrepreneurship*, 166, 157–166

CHUKWU, G. C., TOM, M. C. 2020. Relationship marketing and consumer buying behavior in food and beverage firms in port harcourt metropolis. Middle European Scientific Bulletin, 1(7), 65–76.

CHURCHES, R., WEST-BURNHAM, J. 2008. Leading learning through relationships: The implications of Neuro-linguistic programming for personalisation and the children's agenda in England Welcome to CfBT Education Trust. Online Submission (Eric Database).

IBRAHIM, A, S. 2011. Gangguan Alam Perasaan; Manik depresi, edisi pertama Tanggerang: Jelajah Nusa.

ISA, S. M., MANSOR, A. A., RAZALI, K. 2019. Ethics in Neuromarketing and its implications on business to stay vigilant. KnE Social Sciences, 687–711.

JANG, S., NAMKUNG, Y. 2009. Perceived quality, emotions, and behavioral intentions: Application of an extended mehrabian-russel model to restaurants. Journal of Business Research, 62(4), 451–460.

JENKINS, G. N., DAWES, C. 1964. The effects of different stimuli on the composition of saliva in man. The Journal of Physiology, 170(1), 86–100.

JESENSKÝ, D. a kol. 2018. Marketingová komunikace místě prodeje. POP – POPS, In-store shopper marketing. Praha: Grada Publishing. ISBN 978-80-271-0252-5.

JU, J., AHN, J. H. 2016. The effect of social and ambient factors on impulse purchasing behavior in social commerce. Journal of Organizational Computing and Electronic Commerce, 26(4), 285–306.

KABLE, J. W. 2011. The cognitive neuroscience toolkit for the neuroeconomist. Journal of Neuroscience, Psychology, and Economics, 4(2), 63–84.

KARMARKAR, U. R., SHIV, B., KNUTSON, B. 2015. Cost conscious? The neural and behavioral impact of price primacy on decision making. Journal of Marketing Research, 52(4), 467–481.

KARPOVA, S. V., ROZHKOV, I. V., USTINOVA, O. E. 2019. Neurolinguistic and neuromarketing effects on consumer behavior. Proceedings of the International Scientific and Practical Conference on Digital Economy (ISCDE 2019), 149–154.

KENNING, P., PLASSMANN, H. 2005. NeuroEconomics: An overview from an economic perspective. Brain Research Bulletin, 67(5), 343–354.

KHELEROVÁ, V. 2010. Komunikační a obchodní dovednosti manažera. Praha: Grada Publishing. ISBN 978-80-247-3566-5.

KITA, J. a kol. 2005. Marketing. Bratislava: Iura Edition. 432 s. ISBN 80-8078-049-8.

KITA, J. a kol. 2010. Marketing. 1.vyd. Bratislava: Iura Edition. 411 s. ISBN 978-80-8078-327-3.

KLIMEŠ, J. 2001. Oční kamera a její využití v marketingu. Strategie 9/12. [online]. [cit. 2022-01-03]. Dostupné z: http://klimes.mysteria.cz/clanky/ psychologie/ ocnikamera_marketing.pdf

KNIGHT, S. 2004. Tehnicile programării neuro-lingvistice. Bucuresti: Ed. Curtea Veche.

KNIGHT, S. 2015. NLP v praxi Neurolingvistické programování jako cesta k osobní jedinečnosti. Praha: Management Press. ISBN 978-80-726-1337-3.

KNUTSON, B., GREER, S. M. 2008. Anticipatory affect: Neural correlates and consequences for choice. Philosophical Transactions of the Royal Society B: Biological Sciences, 363(1511), 3771–3786.

KNUTSON, B., RICK, S., WIMMER, G. E., PRELEC, D., LOEWENSTEIN, G. 2007. Neural predictors of purchases. Neuron, 53(1), 147–156.

KOMÁRKOVÁ, R., RYMEŠ, M., VYSEKALOVÁ, J. 1993. Základy psychologie trhu. 1. vyd. Praha: Grada Publishing. ISBN 80-857-8722-9.

KOTLER, P. 1995. Marketing management. Prel. Václav Dolanský. Praha: Victoria Publishing, 1995. Preklad z anglického originálu Marketing Management. 789 s. ISBN 80-85605-08-2.

KOTLER, P. 2013. Marketing management. Praha: Grada Publishing.

KOTLER, P., ARMSTRONG, G. 2004. Marketing. Praha: Grada Publishing. 855s. ISBN 80-247-0513-3.

KOTLER, P., ARMSTRONG, G. 2007. Marketing. 4.vyd. Praha: Grada Publishing. ISBN 80-247-0513-3 13.

KOTLER, P., KELLER, K. L. 2013. Marketing. 14. vyd. Praha: Grada Publishing. ISBN 978-80-247-4150-5.

KOUKOLÍK, F. 2010. Lidství: neuronální koreláty. Praha: Galén.

KOUTNÁ, M. 2017. Emoční inteligence rozumíte svým zákazníkum? Část 1 [online]. 2017, [cit. 2012-01-10]. Dostupné na internete: <https://webovy-ser vis.cz/emocni-inteligence-rozumite-svym-zakaznikum>.

KOVAĽOVÁ, J., BIRKNEROVÁ, Z. 2018. Determinanty obchodného správania z pohľadu obchodníkov a zákazníkov. Prešov: Vydavateľstvo Prešovskej univerzity. ISBN 978-80-555-2177-0.

KOVANDA, L. 2013. Prečo je vzduch zadarmo a panenstvo drahé. Bratislava: Premedia Group, s. r. o. ISBN 987-80-89594-44-3

KOZEL, R. 2006. Moderní marketingový výzkum: nové trendy, kvantitativní a kvalitativní metody a techniky, průběh a organizace, aplikace v praxi, přínosy a možnosti. Praha: Grada Publishing. ISBN 978-80-247-6978-3.

KOZEL, R., MLYNÁŘOVÁ, L., SVOBODOVÁ, H. 2011. Moderní metody a techniky marketingového výzkumu. Praha: Grada Publishing. ISBN 978-80-247-3527-6.

KRETTER, A. et al. 2007. Marketing. Nitra: SPU, 2007. 287 s. ISBN 978-80-8069-849-2.

KRISHNA, A. 2011. Sensory marketing: Research on the sensuality of products. New York: Taylor & Francis Group, Ltd. ISBN 978-1-84169-889-2

KRISHNA, A. 2013. Customer Sense. How the 5 Senses Influence Buying Behavior. Palgrave MacMillan, New York.

KRISHNA, A. 2012. An integrative review of sensory marketing: Engaging the senses to affect perception, judgment and behavior. Journal of Consumer Psychology, 22(3), 332–351.

KRISHNA, A. 2010. Sensory marketing: Research on the sensuality of products. New York: Routledge. ISBN 184169889X.

KRISHNA, A., AHLUWALIA, R. 2008. Language choice in advertising to bilinguals: Asymmetric effects for multinationals versus local firms. The Journal of Consumer Research, 35(4), 692–705.

KRISHNA, A., LWIN, M. O., MORRIN, M. 2010. Product scent and memory. Journal of Consumer Research, 37(1), 57–67.

KRISHNA, A., MORRIN, M. 2008. Does touch affect taste? The perceptual transfer of product container haptic cues. Journal of Consumer Research, 34, 807–818.

KRISHNA, A., MORRIN, M., SAYIN, E. 2014. Smellizing cookies and salivating: A focus on olfactory imagery. Journal of Consumer Research, 41(1), 18–34.

KULIŠŤÁK, P. 2003. Neuropsychologie. Praha: Portál. ISBN 80-7178-554-7.

LAHNEROVÁ, D. 2009. Asertivita pro manažery. Praha: Grada Publishing. ISBN 978-80-247-2892-6.

LAHNEROVÁ, D. 2012. Asertivita pro manažéry. Praha: Grada Publishing, ISBN 978-80-247-4406-3.

LEDERMAN, S. J., KLATZKY, R. L. 2009. Haptic perception: A tutorial. Atten. Percept. Psychophys, 71(7), 1439–1459.

LEE, N. B., BRODERICK, A. J., CHAMBERLAIN L. 2007. What is 'neuromarketing'? A discussion and agenda for furture research. International Journal of Psychophysiology, 63(2), 199–204.

LELKOVÁ, A. 2014. Prejavy asertívneho správania manažéra v manažérskej práci. 1. vyd. Prešov: Bookman, s.r.o. ISBN 978-80-8165-084-0.

LELKOVÁ, A., GBUROVÁ, J. 2015. Asertivita v nákupnom správaní. 1. vyd. Prešov: Bookman, s. r. o. ISBN 978-80-8165-106-9.LENCH, H. C., DARBOR, K. E., BERG, L. A. 2013. Functional perspectives on emotion, behavior, and cognition. Behavioral Sciences, 3(4), 536–540.

LIMBECK, M. 2012. Jak myslí špičkový obchodník. Co odlišuje ty nejlepší od průměr-ných. Praha: Grada Publishing. ISBN 978-80-247-4067-6.

LINDSTRÖM, M. 2009. Nákupologie: pravda a lži o tom, proč nakupujeme. Vyd. 1. Brno: Computer Press. ISBN 978-80-251-2396-6.

LINDSTRÖM, M. 2010. Brand sense: Sensory secrets behind the stuff we buy. New York: Simon & Schuster. Inc. ISBN 978-1-4391-7201-8.

LISÝ, J. a kol. 2005. Ekonómia v novej ekonomike. Bratislava: Iura Edition. ISBN 80-8078-063-3.

LORINCZ, T. 2009. Etika. [online]. [cit. 2021-01-13]. Dostupné z: <http://toml ery.txt.cz/clanky/61952/zsv-22b>.

LUBECK, W. 1996. Základní kniha spirituálni NLP. Praha: PRAGMA. ISBN 80-7205-049-4.

LUNA, F., MACKLIN, R. 2012. Research involving human beings, vulnerability and exploitation. In H. Kuhse, & P. Singer (Eds.), A companion to bioethics (pp. 459-468). Hoboken: Wiley Blackwell.

LWIN, M. O., MORRIN, M., KRISHNA, A. 2010. Exploring the superadditive effects of scent and pictures on verbal recall: An extension of dual coding theory. Journal of Consumer Psychology, 20(3), 317-326.

MACINNIS, D. J., PARK, C. W. 1991. The differential role of characteristics of music on high- and low-involvement consumers' processing of ads. The Journal of Consumer Research, 18, 161-173.

MAJBA, L. 2018. Neuromarketing a jeho využitie v praxi. [online]. [cit. 2022-01-13]. Dostupné z: <http://digibrand.sk/neuromarketing-jeho-vyuzitie-v-praxi/>.

MANDEL, N., JOHNSON, E. J. 2002. When web pages influence choice: Effects of visual primes on experts and novices. Journal of Consumer Research, 29(2), 235-245.

MATTILA, A. S., WIRTZ, J. 2001. Congruency of scent and music as a driver of in-store evaluations and behavior. Journal of Retail, 77, 273-289.

MATÚŠ, J. 2011. Marketing – Významný nástroj zvyšovania konkurencieschopnosti. In Nové trendy v marketingovej komunikácii. Trnava: Fakulta masmediálnej komunikácie Univerzita sv. Cyrila a Metoda v Trnave. ISBN 978-80-8105-335-1.

McDANIEL, C. 1977. Convenience food packaging and the perception of product quality. J. Mark. 41, 57-58.

McDERMOTT, I., JAGO, W. 2006. The coaching Bible: The essential handbook. London: Piatkus.

MEYERS-LEVY, J., PERACCHIO, L. A. 1995. Understanding the effects of color: How the correspondence between available and required resources affects attitudes. Journal of Consumer Research, 22(2), 121-138.

MILLIMAN, R. E. 1982. Using background music to affect the behavior of supermarket shoppers. Journal of Marketing, 46(3), 86-91.

MIŠÍK, M. 2016. O úspechu obchodníka v dnešnej dobe rozhodujú štyri vnútorné kvality. Viete, ktoré sú to? [online]. [cit. 2020-11-09]. Dostupné z: https://www.ezisk.sk/cla-nok/aku-vybavu-potrebuje-moderny-obchodnik-moderny-obchodnik-ivcast/3395/?fbclid=IwAR0v2MhdvAELjsNL08Ir1l yxWdOOs-zOp3WtHgvPZ4TDv1nP4gQVFt-K3mnM

MITCHELL, D. J., KAHN, B. E., KNASKO, S. C. 1995. There's something in the air: Effects of congruent or incongruent ambient odor on consumer decision making. The Journal of Consumer Research, 22(2), 229–238.

MORALES, A. C., FITZSIMONS, G. F. 2007. Product contagion: Changing consumer evaluations through physical contact with "disgusting" products. Journal of Marketing Research, 44, 272–283.

MORHENN, V. B., PARK, J. W., PIPER, E. 2008. Monetary sacrifice among strangers is mediated by endogenous oxytocin release after physical contact. Evolution and Human Behavior, 29(6), 375–383.

MORIN, C. 2011a. Neuromarketing: The new science of consumer behavior. Society, 48(2), 131–135.

MORIN, C. 2011b. Neuromarketing: The new science of consumer behavior. Symposium: Consumer Culture in Global Perspective, 48, 131–135.

MORRIS, R. 2003. Neuroscience – Science of the brain. Liverpool: British Neuroscience Association.

MUNCY, J. A. 1996. Measuring perceived brand parity. ACR North American Advances, 23, 411–417.

MURPHY, E. a kol. 2008. Neuroethics of neuromarketing. Journal of Consumer Behavior, 7, 293–302. [online]. [cit. 2021-01-06]. Dostupné z: <https://onlinelibrary.wiley.com/doi/pdf/10.1002/cb.250>.

MÜLLER K. 2019. Further services. [online]. [cit. 2022-01-13]. Dostupné z: <https://www.neuromarketing-labs.com/services/further-services/>.

NEDERKOORN, C., SMULDERS, F., JANSEN, A. 2000. Cephalic phase responses, craving, and food intake in normal subjects. Appetite, 35(1), 45–55.

NEMEROFF, C. J., ROZIN, P. 1994. The contagion concept in adult thinking in the United States: Transmission of germs and of interpersonal influence. Ethos. Journal of the Society for Psychological Anthropology, 22, 158–186

NEVŠÍMALOVÁ, S., RŮŽIČKA, E., TICHÝ, J. 2002. Neurologie. Praha: Galén.

NÍZKA, H. 2007. Aplikovaný marketing. Bratislava: Iura Edition, s. r.o. ISBN: 978-80-8078-157-6

NORTH, A. C. 2012. The effect of background music on the taste of wine. The British Journal of Psychology, 103(3), 293–301.

NORTH, A. C., HARGREAVES, D. J., MCKENDRICK, J. 1999. The influence of in-store music on wine selections. The Journal of Applied Psychology, 84(2), 271-276.

OLÁH, Ľ., FOGAŠOVÁ, V. 2013. Neuromarketing – revolúcia v skúmaní správania spotrebiteľa? [online]. [cit. 2021-10-13]. Dostupné z: <http:// www.ruonline.sk/neuromarketing-%E2%80%93-revolucia-v-skumani-spravania-spotrebitela/>.

OUPIC, M. 2008. Neuro-lingvistické programování [online]. 2008, [cit. 2021-06-09]. Dostupné na internete: <http://www.marketingovenoviny.cz/ marketing_6806/

O'CONNOR, J., McDERMOTT, I. 2001. The NLP workbook: A practical guide to achieving the results you want. London: Thorsons.

PAGE, G. 2012. Scientific realism: What 'Neuromarketing' can and can't tell us about consumers. USA: International Journal Of Market Research.

PAJONK, P., PLEVOVÁ, K. 2015. Vnemový marketing, zmysly v podpore predaja. Studia commercialia Bratislavensia, 8(29). ISSN 1337-7493.

PALFIOVÁ, A. 2011. Vhodné osvetlenie zatraktívni tovar. [online]. [cit. 2021-10-04]. Dostupné z: http://dennik.hnonline.sk/b2b-211/vhodne-osvetlenie-zatraktivni-tovar-457559

PARK, C. W., JAWORSKI, B. J., MACLNNIS, D. J. 1986. Strategic brand concept-image management. Journal of Marketing, 50(4), 135-145.

PECINA, S., SMITH, K. S. 2010. Hedonic and motivational roles of opioids in food reward: implications for overeating disorders. Pharmacology Biochemistry and Behavior, 97(1), 34-46.

PECK, J., CHILDERS, T. L. 2003. Individual differences in haptic information processing: The "need for touch" scale. Journal of Consumer Research, 30(3), 430-442.

PECK, J., WIGGINS, J. 2006. It just feels good: Customer's affective response to touch and its influence on persuasion. Journal of Marketing. [online], 70(4). ISSN 1547-718.

PENDLETON, D. 2012. Leadership for Primary Health Care Research. Primary Health Care Research & Development, 13(4), 301-307.

PENSIERI, C. 2013. Neurolinguistic programming in health: An analysis of the literature. Medic, 21(2), 97-105

PETTY, R. E., CACIOPPO, J. T. 1983. The role of bodily responses in attitude measurement and change. In J. T. Cacioppo, & R. R. Petty (Eds.), Social psychophysiology: A sourcebook. New York, NY: Guilford Press.

PLASSMANN, H., O'DOHERTY, J., RANGEL, A. 2007. Orbitofrontal cortex encodes willingness to pay in everyday economic transactions. *J Neurosci* 27(37). 9984–9988.

PLASSMANN, H., RAMSØY, T. Z., MILOSAVLJEVIC, M. 2012. Branding the brain: A critical review and outlook. Journal of Consumer Psychology, 22(1), 18–36.

PLESSIS, E. 2011. The branded mind: What neuroscience really tell us about the puzzle of the brain and the brand. London: Kogan Page. ISBN 978-07-494-6125-6.

PODANÁ, R. 2012. Koučování pro manažery. Grada Publishing.

PRAGHOLAPATI, A. 2019. The effect of brain gym to the level of depression in geriatric at balai perlindungan sosial tresna werdha ciparay bandung. Jurnal Skolastik Keperawatan, 5(2), 128 –146.

RAAB, G., ELGER, C. E., NEUNER, M., WEBER, B. 2011. A neurological study of compulsive buying behaviour. Journal of Consumer Policy, 34(4), 401.

RAGHUBIR, P., KRISHNA, A. 1999. Vital dimensions in volume perception: Can the eye fool the stomach? Journal of Marketing Research, 36(3), 313–326.

REBEŤÁK, J. 2016. Ovplyvňovanie pacientov. In Medium [online]. 2016, č. 1, [cit. 2021-01-23]. s. 26–27. Dostupné na internete: <https://www.med-art.sk/buxus/docs/medium/Medium-1-2016_40_stran-web.pdf>.

REIMANN, M., ZAICHKOWSKY, J., NEUHAUS, C., BENDER, T., WEBER, B. 2010. Aesthetic package design: A behavioral, neural, and psychological investigation. Journal of Consumer Psychology, 20(4), 431–441.

RICHTEROVÁ, K. et al. (1993). A collection of examples from marketing. Bratislava: Edition Center, University of Economics.

RIZA, A. F., WIJAYANTI, D. 2018. The triangle of sensory marketing model: Does it stimulate brand experience and loyalty. Esensi: Jurnal Bisnis dan Manajemen, 8(1), 57–66.

ROSEN, S. 1991. My Voice will Go with You, W.W.Norton, New York, NY.

ROTH V. A. 2013. The potential of neuromarketing as a marketing tool. 1st IBA Bachelor Thesis Conference, Enschede.

ROZIN, P., NEMEROFF, C. 1990. The laws of sympathetic magic in disgust and other domains. Cultural Psychology (pp. 205–232). Cambridge, UK: Cambridge Univ. Press.

RANDHIR, R. a kol. 2016. Analyzing the Impact of Sensory Marketing on Consumers: A Case Study of KFC. In Journal of US-China Public Administration. Vol. 13, No 4. ISSN 278-292.

SAELAN, A., PURWARIANTI, A. 2013. Generating mind map from Indonesian text using natural language processing tools. Procedia Technology, 11, 1163–1169.

SAMUHELOVÁ, M., ŠIMKOVÁ, L. 2015. Neuromarketing. Úvod do problematiky. Časť I. [online]. 2015, [cit. 2021-01-10]. Dostupné na internete: <https://www.mins.sk/neuromarketing-uvod-problematiky/>.

SEDLÁKOVÁ, M. 2004. Vybrané kapitoly z kognitivní psychologie: Mentální reprezentace a mentální modely. 1. vyd. Praha: Grada Publishing. ISBN 80-247-0375-0.

SENGUPTA, J., GORN, G. J. 2002. Absence makes the mind grow sharper: Effects of element omission on subsequent recall. Journal of Marketing Research, 39(2), 186–201.

SCHAFER, A., 2005. Buy this. Scientific American Mind, 16(2), 72–75.

SCHIFFMAN, L. G., KANUK, L. L. 2004. Nákupní chování. Brno: Computer Press. ISBN 80-251-0094-4.

SCHMITT, B. H. 1999. Experiential marketing: How to get customers to sense, feel, think, act, relate to your company and brands. New York, NY: The Free Press.

SIKELA, H. 2014. Zmyslový marketing. [online]. [cit. 2021-10-18]. Dostupné z: http://www.ta3.com/clanok/1041008/zmyslovymarketing.html

SINGER, E. 2004. They know what you want--if neuromarketers can find the key to our consumer desires, will they be able to manipulate what we buy?. New Scientist, 183(2458), 36–37.

SLOWTHER, A., KLEINMAN, I. 2009. Confidentiality. In P. Singer, & A. M. Viens (Eds.), Cambridge textbook of bioethics (pp. 43–48). Cambridge, MA: Cambridge University Press.

SOLNAIS, C., ANDREU-PEREZ, J., SÁNCHEZ-FERNÁNDEZ, J., ANDRÉU-ABELA, J. 2013. The contribution of neuroscience to consumer research: A conceptual framework and empirical review. Journal of Economic Psychology, 36, 68–81.

SOMERVUORI, O., RAVAJA, N. 2013. Purchase behavior and psychophysiological responses to different price levels. Psychology and Marketing, 30(6), 479–489.

SOUSA, J. 2018. Neuromarketing and big data analytics for strategic consumer engagment: Emerging research and opportunities. United States of America: IGI Global. ISBN 978-15-225-4834-8.

SRPOVÁ, J. a kol. 2010. Základy podnikání. Praha: Grada Publishing. ISBN 978-80-247-3339-5.

STILLMAN, J. A. 2002. Gustation: Intersensory experience par excellence. Perception, 31(12), 1491–1500.

STOLL, M., BAECKE, S., KENNING, P. 2008. What they see is what they get? An fMRI-study on neural correlates of attractive packaging. Journal of Consumer Behaviour, 7(4–5), 342–359.

STOUT, P., LECKENBY, J. D. 1988. Let the music play: Music as a nonverbal element in television commercials. In S. Hecker, & D. W. Stewart (Eds.), Nonverbal communication in advertising (pp. 207–233). Lexington, MA: Lexington Books.

STURT, J., ALI, S., ROBERTSON, W., METCALFE, D., GROVE, A., BOURNE, C., BRIDLE, C. 2012. Neuro-linguistic programming: A systematic review of the effects on health outcomes. British Journal of General Practice, 62(604), 757–764.

SZARKOVÁ, M. 2000. Psychológia: základy ekonomickej psychológie. Bratislava: Ekonóm. ISBN 80-225-1093-9.

SZARKOVÁ, M. 2007. Psychológia pre manažérov a podnikateľov. Bratislava: SPRINT. ISBN 80-89085-77-6.

ŠÁŠIKOVÁ, M. 2013. Neuromarketing na Slovensku a v zahraničí a jeho etické aspekty. Bratislava: Ekonomická univerzita v Bratislave, Obchodná fakulta. [online]. [cit. 2021-12-12]. Dostupné na internete: <http://www.cutn.sk/Library/proceedings/mch_2013/editovane_prispevky/42.%20%C5%A0%C3%A1%C5%A1ikov%C3%A1.pdf>.

ŠIKL, R. 2012. Zrakové vnímání. Praha: Grada Publishing.

ŠTIBINGER, A. 2010. Vůně jako nástroj smyslového marketingu [online]. [cit. 2021-11-09]. Dostupné z: http://www.dmarketing.cz/2010/07/vune-jako-nastroj-smyslovehomarketingu/

ŠULEŘ, O. 2008. 5 rolí manažera a jak je profesionálne zvládnout. Praha: Computer Press. ISBN 978-80-251-2316-4.

ŠVEC, M. 2014. O nás [online]. 2014, [cit. 2021-11-11]. Dostupné na internete: <http://neuromarketing.sk/?page_id=15>.

TANAKA, G., OGAWA, T., INADOMI, H., KIKUCHI, Y., OHTA, Y. 2003. Effects of an educational program on public attitudes towards mental illness. Psychiatry and Clinical Neurosciences, 57(6), 595–602.

TÁBORECKÁ-PETROVIČOVÁ, J. 2011. Modely spotrebiteľského správania sociálnych tried pri tvorbe marketingovej stratégie. Bratislava: Iura Edition. ISBN 978-80-8078-398-3.

THOMAS, A. a kol. 2017. Ethics and neuromarketing: Implications for market researhc and business practice. Berlín: Springer. ISBN 978-3-319-45607-2.

TOMAŠOVIČ, P. 2015. Neurolingvistické programovanie v praxi manažéra [online]. 2015, [cit. 2021-01-10]. Dostupné na internete: <http://www.vianova.sk/2015/11/02/neurolingvisticke-programovanie-v-praxi-manazera/>.

TOMEK, G. 2011. Marketing od myšlenky k realizaci. Praha: Professional Publishing.

TREBUŇA, P. a kol. 2007. Vybrané kapitoly z marketingu 1. Košice: Technická univerzita v Košiciach. Strojnícka fakulta. ISBN 978-80-8073-881-5.

TYRLÍKOVÁ, I., BAREŠ, M., BALÁŽ, M., BRÁZDIL, M. BRICHTA, J., DUFEK, J., DUFEK, M., HUMMELOVÁ, Z., CHRASTINA, J. MIKULÍK, R., MINKS, E., MUCHOVÁ, M., NOVÁK, Z., REKTOR, I., REKTOROVÁ, I. 2012. Neurologie pro nelékařské obory. Brno: Národní centrum ošetřovatelství a nelékařských zdravotnických oborů.

UDO-IMEH, P. 2022. Personality and consumer behaviour: A review. European Journal of Business and Management. [online]. [cit. 2021-11-07]. Dostupné z: https://www.academia.edu/71872666/ Personality_and_Consumer_Behaviour_A_Review

ULMAN, Y. I., CAKAR, T., YILDIZ, G. 2015. Ethical issues in neuromarketing: "I consume, therefore I am!". Science and Engineering Ethics, 21(5), 1271–1284.

VASIĽOVÁ, M., DRAŽOVÁ, K. 2015. Neuromarketing as a modern way to understand consumer behavior. *In*: Current challenges of marketing and their application in practice: scientific states: [proceedings]: International scientific event, 15.10.2010 in Bratislava. Bratislava: EKONÓM EU Publishing House. pp. 176-183. ISBN 978-80- 225-3037-8.

VÁLEK, V. 1998. Moderní diagnostické metody, II. díl výpočetní tomografie. Brno: IDVPZ.

VÁLEK, V., ŽIŽKA, J. 1996. Moderní diagnostické metody, III. díl magnetická rezonance. Brno: Institut pro další vzdělávání pracovníků ve zdravotnictví, Vol. 27, No. 7–8, 854–868.

VECCHIATO, G., TOPPI, J., ASTOLFI, L., FALLANI, F. D. V., CINCOTTI, F., MATTIA, D., BABILONI, F. 2011. Spectral EEG frontal asymmetries correlate with the experienced pleasantness of TV commercial advertisements. Medical & Biological Engineering & Computing, 49(5), 579–583.

VERYZER, J. R., HUTCHINSON, J. W. 1998. The influence of unity and prototypicality on aesthetic responses to new product designs. Journal of Consumer Research, 24(4), 374–385.

VESECKÝ, Z. 2015. Vyzkoušejte aroma marketing. Váš úspěch je ve vzduchu. [online]. [cit. 2021-12-10]. Dostupné z: http://www.podnikatel. cz/clanky/vyzkousejte-aroma-marketing-vasuspech-je-ve-vzduchu/

VIESTOVÁ, K. a kol. 2006. Lexikón obchodu (1): Trh, obchod, tovar. Bratislava: Ekonóm. ISBN 80-225-2131-0.

VYSEKALOVÁ, J. 2011. Chování zákazníka: jak odkrýt tajemství "černé skříňky". 1. vyd. Praha: Grada Publishing. ISBN 978-80-247-3528-3.

VYSEKALOVÁ, J. 2012. Psychologie reklamy. 4. rozš. a aktualiz. vyd. Praha: Grada Publishing. ISBN 978-80-247-4005-8.

VYSEKALOVÁ, J. 2014. Emoce v marketingu: jak oslovit srdce zákazníka. Praha: Grada Publishing. ISBN 978-80-2474-843-6.

WAKE, L. 2008. Neurolinguistic psychotherapy: A postmodern perspective. London: Routledge.

WALTON, C. 2004. The brave new world of neuromarketing is here. B&T (Australia), November 19, p. 22.

WANG, Y. M., ELHAG, T. 2008. An adaptive neuro-fuzzy inference system for bridge risk assessment. Expert Systems with Applications, 34(4), 3099–3106.

WEITZENHOFFER, A. 1989. The practice of hypnotism volume 2: Applications of traditional an semi-traditional hypnotism. Non-traditional hypnotism. New York: John Wiley & Sons, In.

WILSON R. M. a kol. 2008. Neuromarketing and Consumer Free Will. Journal of Consumer Affairs, 42(3), 389–410. ISSN 0022-0078.

WILSON, R., GAINES, J., HILL, R. P. 2008. Neuromarketing and consumer free will. Journal of Consumer Affairs, 42(3), 389–410.

WITOWSKI, T. 2012. A Review of Research Findings on Neuro-Linguistic Programming. The Scientific Review of Mental Health Practice 9, 29–40.

WOLFE, J. M., KLUENDER, K. R., LEVI, D. M., BARTOSHUK, L. M., HERZ, R. S., KLATZKY, R. L. et al. 2006. Sensation & perception. Sunderland, MA: Sinauer Associates.

WYSOCKI, C. J., PELCHAT, M. L. 1993. The effects of aging on the human sense of smell and its relationship to food choice. Critical Reviews in Food Science and Nutrition, 33(1), 63–82.

YALCH, R. F., SPANGENBERG, E. R. 2000. The effects of music in a retail setting on real and perceived shopping times. Journal of Business Research, 49(2), 139–147.

YAMAZAKI, H. 2007. Nlpno Kihonga Wakaruhon [Understanding the Basic of NLP]. Tokyo: Japan Management Center.

YANUARITA, F. A. 2012. Memaksimalkan Otak Melalui Senam Otak (Brain Gym). Yogyakarta: Teranova Books.

YORKSTON, E. 2010. Auxiliary auditory ambitions: Assessing ancillary and ambient sounds. In A. Krishna (Ed.), Sensory marketing: Research on the sensuality of products. New York, NY: Routledge.

YUAN, Y., CHEN, X., SUN, Q. 2017. A stock market model based on the interaction of heterogeneous traders' behavior. In D. N. Cassenti (Ed.), Advances in human factors in simulation and modeling (pp. 312–321). Cham: Springer International Publishing. ISBN 978-3-319-60590-6.

ZAMAZALOVÁ, M. 2009. Marketing obchodní firmy. 1. vyd. Praha: Grada Publishing. ISBN 978-80-247-2049-4.

ZAMFIR, C. M. a kol. 2013. The NLP logical levels of culture: A business perspective. Studia Universitatis Babes-Bolyai-Philologia, 58(2), 139–151.

ZAMPINI, M., WANTLING, E., PHILLIPS, N., SPENCE, C. 2008. Multisensory flavor perception: Assessing the influence of fruit acids and color cues on the perception of fruit-flavored beverages. Food Quality and Preference, 19(3), 335–343.

ZAMPINI, M., SPENCE, C. 2004. The role of auditory cues in modulating the perceived crispness and staleness of potato chips. Journal of Sensory Science, 19, 347–363.

ZARANTONELLO, L., SCHMITT, B. H. 2010. Using the brand experience scale to profile consumers and predict consumer behavior. Journal of Brand Management, 17(7), 532–540.

ZHU, R., MEYERS-LEVY, J. 2005. Distinguishing between the meanings of music: When background music affects product perceptions. Journal of Marketing Research, 42(3), 333–345

ZURAWICKI, L. 2010. Neuromarketng: Exploring the brain of the consumer. Berlin: Springer.

SM-CEB
Sensory marketing – cognitions, emotions, behavior

(Birknerová, Miško, Ondrijová, 2022)

Please read each statement and indicate how well it corresponds to your way of responding. Indicate your answer by crossing out the chosen number on a scale from 1 to 6.

1	2	3	4	5	6
absolutely no	no	no more than yes	yes more than no	yes	definitely yes

1.	Product information must be accompanied by pleasant music.	1	2	3	4	5	6
2.	When a customer enters a store and hears music in the background, it evokes pleasant emotions.	1	2	3	4	5	6
3.	When a customer hears a song by a favorite artist in a shopping mall, it influences his shopping behavior.	1	2	3	4	5	6
4.	It is important for the customer to know that he can hold the product in his own hands.	1	2	3	4	5	6
5.	When a customer holds a product while buying something, it creates positive emotions in him.	1	2	3	4	5	6
6.	When buying a product, the customer needs to verify the quality of its processing by touch.	1	2	3	4	5	6
7.	When buying a product, its scent is important information for the customer.	1	2	3	4	5	6
8.	When a customer makes a purchase, the pleasant scent in the store evokes positive emotions.	1	2	3	4	5	6
9.	A pleasant scent can influence the customer's business behavior.	1	2	3	4	5	6
10.	If the customer may taste the product, it is important information for him.	1	2	3	4	5	6
11.	If the customer has the opportunity to taste the product, it evokes positive emotions in him.	1	2	3	4	5	6
12.	When a customer tastes a new type of product in a store, it may influence him sufficiently to buy it.	1	2	3	4	5	6
13.	When buying a product, its description and composition on the packaging are important for the customer.	1	2	3	4	5	6
14.	When buying a product, attractive packaging evokes positive emotions in the customer.	1	2	3	4	5	6
15.	The packaging of the product greatly influences the decision to buy it.	1	2	3	4	5	6

DOBB – T
Determinants of business behavior – *trader*

(Birknerová, Kovaľová, 2020)

Please read each statement and indicate how well it corresponds to your way of responding. Indicate your answer by crossing out the chosen number on a scale from 1 to 6.

1	2	3	4	5	6
absolutely no	no	no more than yes	yes more than no	yes	definitely yes

1.	I feel like I'm manipulating customers.	1	2	3	4	5	6
2.	I use manipulative techniques when selling.	1	2	3	4	5	6
3.	I can recognize my manipulative behavior.	1	2	3	4	5	6
4.	Customers know how to defend against my manipulative behavior.	1	2	3	4	5	6
5.	Customers know how to react to my manipulative behavior.	1	2	3	4	5	6
6.	My manipulative behavior discourages customers from buying products.	1	2	3	4	5	6
7.	I don't mind manipulative behavior towards customers.	1	2	3	4	5	6
8.	I perceive manipulative behavior as part of the sales process.	1	2	3	4	5	6
9.	When I am manipulative, I feel negative emotions.	1	2	3	4	5	6
10.	When customers feel manipulated by me, they won't come back next time.	1	2	3	4	5	6
11.	I always sell only what the customer wants.	1	2	3	4	5	6
12.	Customers will not let be manipulated by my tactics.	1	2	3	4	5	6
13.	When I am involved in sales, I motivate customers to buy products faster.	1	2	3	4	5	6
14.	If I provide the customer with quality information about the product, its value also increases for the customer.	1	2	3	4	5	6
15.	With my positive attitude, I can change the customer's choice of product.	1	2	3	4	5	6
16.	When choosing a product, customers ask for advice when I am engaged.	1	2	3	4	5	6
17.	An engaged trader is an added value for business these days.	1	2	3	4	5	6
18.	I positively assess the high involvement of the trader.	1	2	3	4	5	6
19.	When shopping, customers always have enough essential information about products from me.	1	2	3	4	5	6

20.	I feel better about sales when I have an engaged approach to the customer.	1	2	3	4	5	6
21.	If I don't take care of customers, they leave the store.	1	2	3	4	5	6
22.	If I ignore the customer, he looks for a competing store.	1	2	3	4	5	6
23.	When I am engaged, customer satisfaction motivates them to repeat purchases.	1	2	3	4	5	6
24.	If I take care of the customer, he is willing to pay a higher price for the product.	1	2	3	4	5	6
25.	If the customer sees that I am in a stressful situation, he takes me into account.	1	2	3	4	5	6
26.	Customers try to understand me when I'm stressed.	1	2	3	4	5	6
27.	Customers respect me when I am under stress, I have a right to that.	1	2	3	4	5	6
28.	Customers often observe my expressions of stress.	1	2	3	4	5	6
29.	Customers don't like it when I show signs of stress to them.	1	2	3	4	5	6
30.	Customers don't like it when I confess my problems to them.	1	2	3	4	5	6
31.	In a store where the customer feels stressed, he does not feel comfortable.	1	2	3	4	5	6
32.	When shopping, customers require a calm atmosphere from me.	1	2	3	4	5	6
33.	Customers get nervous when I serve them under stress.	1	2	3	4	5	6
34.	When I'm stressed customers overlook me while shopping.	1	2	3	4	5	6
35.	Customers can tell when I'm under stress.	1	2	3	4	5	6
36.	The stress of shopping drives customers crazy.	1	2	3	4	5	6
37.	Customers appreciate it when I give them an honest opinion about a product.	1	2	3	4	5	6
38.	Customers appreciate it if I listen carefully to their requests.	1	2	3	4	5	6
39.	It is suitable if I make sure that I understood the customer's request correctly.	1	2	3	4	5	6
40.	If the customer is critical of the product offering, I can accept his criticism.	1	2	3	4	5	6
41.	If the customer is dissatisfied with the purchase, I ask him how I could meet his request.	1	2	3	4	5	6
42.	Customers appreciate it when I can decently defend myself against unjustified criticism.	1	2	3	4	5	6
43.	Customers appreciate it if I make sure I understood their requests.	1	2	3	4	5	6

44.	Customers appreciate it if I start the conversation with them first.	1	2	3	4	5	6
45.	Customers feel good if I genuinely flatter them while shopping without ulterior motives.	1	2	3	4	5	6
46.	Customers appreciate when I keep my emotions under control.	1	2	3	4	5	6
47.	Customers have a better shopping experience if I respect their opinion about the product.	1	2	3	4	5	6
48.	Customers appreciate it if I don't apologize for things beyond my control.	1	2	3	4	5	6

DOBB – C
Determinants of business behavior – *customer*

(Birknerová, Kovaľová, 2020)

Please read each statement and indicate how well it corresponds to your way of responding. Indicate your answer by crossing out the chosen number on a scale from 1 to 6.

1 absolutely no	2 no	3 no more than yes	4 yes more than no	5 yes	6 definitely yes

1.	When shopping, I feel manipulated by a trader.	1	2	3	4	5	6
2.	When shopping, I feel the manipulative behavior of traders.	1	2	3	4	5	6
3.	I can recognize the manipulative behavior of traders.	1	2	3	4	5	6
4.	I know how to defend against manipulative behavior in the store.	1	2	3	4	5	6
5.	I know how to respond suitably to manipulative behavior in the store.	1	2	3	4	5	6
6.	The manipulative behavior of the salesman discourages me from buying products.	1	2	3	4	5	6
7.	I don't mind the manipulative behavior of traders.	1	2	3	4	5	6
8.	I perceive manipulative behavior as part of the sales process.	1	2	3	4	5	6
9.	When I feel manipulated in a store, I feel unpleasant emotions.	1	2	3	4	5	6
10.	When I feel manipulated in a store, next time I won't come.	1	2	3	4	5	6
11.	I always buy only what I want.	1	2	3	4	5	6
12.	I will not be manipulated by the tactics of salesmen.	1	2	3	4	5	6
13.	In the store, an engaged salesperson motivates me to buy products faster.	1	2	3	4	5	6
14.	When a merchant provides me with quality information about a product, its value increases for me.	1	2	3	4	5	6
15.	With a positive attitude, a trader can change a customer's product selection.	1	2	3	4	5	6
16.	When choosing a product, I will accept a piece of advice from an engaged trader.	1	2	3	4	5	6
17.	An engaged trader is the added value for business these days.	1	2	3	4	5	6
18.	I appreciate the high commitment of a trader.	1	2	3	4	5	6
19.	When shopping, I always have enough essential information about products.	1	2	3	4	5	6

20.	I feel better about shopping if a trader is engaged.	1	2	3	4	5	6
21.	If the salesman doesn't pay attention to me, I leave the store.	1	2	3	4	5	6
22.	If a salesperson ignores me in a store, I look for a competing store.	1	2	3	4	5	6
23.	Satisfaction with a committed trader motivates me to repeat purchases.	1	2	3	4	5	6
24.	If a trader devotes me, I am willing to pay a higher price for the product.	1	2	3	4	5	6
25.	If I see that a trader is exposed to a stressful situation, I take him into account.	1	2	3	4	5	6
26.	I try to understand a stressed businessman.	1	2	3	4	5	6
27.	I respect that when a businessman is under stress, he has the right to do so.	1	2	3	4	5	6
28.	I often observe signs of stress in traders.	1	2	3	4	5	6
29.	I don't like it when a salesperson transfers stress to customers.	1	2	3	4	5	6
30.	I don't like it when a businessman confides his problems to me.	1	2	3	4	5	6
31.	I don't feel comfortable in a store where I feel stressed.	1	2	3	4	5	6
32.	I require a calm atmosphere when shopping.	1	2	3	4	5	6
33.	I get nervous when served by a stressed-out salesperson.	1	2	3	4	5	6
34.	When shopping, I don't notice a stressed-out trader.	1	2	3	4	5	6
35.	I can tell when a trader is under stress.	1	2	3	4	5	6
36.	Stress drives me crazy when shopping.	1	2	3	4	5	6
37.	I appreciate it when a trader honestly tells me his opinion about the product.	1	2	3	4	5	6
38.	I appreciate it when a trader listens carefully to my purchase request.	1	2	3	4	5	6
39.	I appreciate it when a trader makes sure that he understands my purchase request correctly.	1	2	3	4	5	6
40.	When I am critical about the product offer, a trader can accept it.	1	2	3	4	5	6
41.	When I am dissatisfied with a purchase, a trader asks me how he could meet my requests.	1	2	3	4	5	6
42.	I appreciate it when a trader knows how to defend himself decently against unjustified criticism.	1	2	3	4	5	6
43.	I evaluate it positively when a trader makes sure that he understood my request.	1	2	3	4	5	6

44.	I appreciate a trader who has no problem starting a conversation with me first.	1	2	3	4	5	6
45.	I feel good when a trader genuinely flatters me while shopping without ulterior motives	1	2	3	4	5	6
46.	I appreciate it if the trader has his emotions fully under control.	1	2	3	4	5	6
47.	I feel better about shopping if a trader respects my opinion about the product.	1	2	3	4	5	6
48.	I appreciate it when a businessman doesn't make excuses for things beyond his control.	1	2	3	4	5	6

The NLP Technique questionnaire (NLP-T)

(Frankovský et al., 2018)

Please read each statement and indicate how well it corresponds to your way of responding. Indicate your answer by crossing out the chosen number on a scale from 0 to 5.

0 definitely not	1 no	2 rather no than yes	3 rather yes than no	4 yes	5 definitely

1.	When communicating with my partner, I use his style of expression.	0	1	2	3	4	5
2.	During the conversation, I listen carefully to what words the partner uses.	0	1	2	3	4	5
3.	When talking with my partner, I carefully observe his eyes.	0	1	2	3	4	5
4.	I use several styles of communication when talking in front of people.	0	1	2	3	4	5
5.	I behave in a way that best suits the other person.	0	1	2	3	4	5
6.	When communicating with my partner, I try to understand how he perceives it.	0	1	2	3	4	5
7.	For the correct understanding of the information, it is important to set a relationship with the partner.	0	1	2	3	4	5
8.	What kind of relationship I have with the given person is important in convincing this person.	0	1	2	3	4	5
9.	Information sharing between people depends on mutual trust.	0	1	2	3	4	5
10.	I communicate better with a person who has the same values, attitudes, and opinions as me.	0	1	2	3	4	5
11.	In persuading someone, I try to make the person change his thinking and behavior.	0	1	2	3	4	5
12.	If I communicate with an upset person, I first get upset, and only after calming down I approach what I want.	0	1	2	3	4	5
13.	Using emotions in communication makes it much easier for me.	0	1	2	3	4	5
14.	First, I try to change my partner's opinion and expect a difference in his behavior.	0	1	2	3	4	5
15.	When communicating, I use my partner's experience, thereby leading him to a new way of thinking about the problem.	0	1	2	3	4	5

The NLP Communication questionnaire (NLP-C)

(Frankovský et al., 2018)

Please read each statement and indicate how well it corresponds to your way of responding. Indicate your answer by crossing out the chosen number on a scale from 0 to 5.

0	1	2	3	4	5
definitely not	no	rather no than yes	rather yes than no	yes	definitely

1.	During the conversation, I observe the body language of my counterpart.	0	1	2	3	4	5
2.	There are situations when I consciously suppress my own negative body language signals.	0	1	2	3	4	5
3.	Body language often tells more about a person's emotions and inner attitudes than spoken language.	0	1	2	3	4	5
4.	The non-verbal accompaniment of my spoken speech follows the rule of the golden mean.	0	1	2	3	4	5
5.	When listening to my partner, I focus on both verbal and non-verbal expressions of his speech.	0	1	2	3	4	5
6.	When listening to the speaker, through my verbal and non-verbal expressions, I show that I perceive him.	0	1	2	3	4	5
7.	Listening is very important for the conversation, so I pay a lot of attention to it.	0	1	2	3	4	5
8.	My listening skills are at a high level.	0	1	2	3	4	5
9.	In communication, I always try to achieve the satisfaction of both parties.	0	1	2	3	4	5
10.	If necessary, I can say no in any situation.	0	1	2	3	4	5
11.	If someone treats me unfairly, I will point it out.	0	1	2	3	4	5
12.	I am honest and straightforward in expressing positive and negative feelings towards the other party.	0	1	2	3	4	5
13.	In communication, I use one of the questioning techniques.	0	1	2	3	4	5
14.	I get accurate information by asking relevant questions.	0	1	2	3	4	5
15.	I ask so that I have an accurate idea of what the communication partner is thinking.	0	1	2	3	4	5
16.	I realize that by asking the wrong questions, I can disrupt communication.	0	1	2	3	4	5
17.	My questioning ability is at a high level.	0	1	2	3	4	5

The Neuromarketing questionnaire (NM-SSP)

(Birknerová, Miško, Tomková, 2022)

Please read each statement and indicate how well it corresponds to your way of responding. Indicate your answer by crossing out the chosen number on a scale from 0 to 5.

0 definitely not	1 no	2 rather no than yes	3 rather yes than no	4 yes	5 definitely

1.	When shopping, store lighting is important to me.	0	1	2	3	4	5
2.	When shopping, the store temperature is important to me.	0	1	2	3	4	5
3.	When shopping, the pleasant scent in the store is important to me.	0	1	2	3	4	5
4.	Pleasant music in the store is important to me when shopping.	0	1	2	3	4	5
5.	The cleanliness of the store is important to me when shopping.	0	1	2	3	4	5
6.	The color of the store's interior is important to me when making a purchase.	0	1	2	3	4	5
7.	The organization of products in the store is important to me when shopping.	0	1	2	3	4	5
8.	The arrangement of the space in the store is important to me when shopping.	0	1	2	3	4	5
9.	The location of the store is important to me when shopping.	0	1	2	3	4	5
10.	The brand of the store is important to me when shopping.	0	1	2	3	4	5
11.	The gender of the seller is important to me when shopping.	0	1	2	3	4	5
12.	The appearance (shape, color) of the seller's corporate clothing is important to me when purchasing.	0	1	2	3	4	5
13.	The cleanliness of the seller's clothes is important to me when making a purchase.	0	1	2	3	4	5
14.	Information from the seller is important to me when shopping.	0	1	2	3	4	5
15.	The physical appearance of the seller is important to me when making a purchase.	0	1	2	3	4	5
16.	The seller's mood is important to me when shopping.	0	1	2	3	4	5
17.	The seller's speech is important to me when making a purchase.	0	1	2	3	4	5
18.	Product recommendation from the seller is important to me when purchasing.	0	1	2	3	4	5
19.	When making a purchase, it is important for me to be addressed by the seller.	0	1	2	3	4	5

20.	The willingness of the seller is important to me when buying.	0	1	2	3	4	5
21.	Participating in contests is important to me when shopping.	0	1	2	3	4	5
22.	A gift with purchase is important to me when shopping.	0	1	2	3	4	5
23.	A discount for the next purchase is important to me when shopping.	0	1	2	3	4	5
24.	The opportunity to try or taste the product is important to me when purchasing.	0	1	2	3	4	5
25.	A stock (special) offer of an unknown product is important to me when purchasing.	0	1	2	3	4	5
26.	A stock (special) offer of an unnecessary product is important to me when purchasing.	0	1	2	3	4	5
27.	Following the price of the product before the discount is important to me when shopping.	0	1	2	3	4	5
28.	Color-different price information about the product is important to me when purchasing.	0	1	2	3	4	5
29.	Visual display of the product in a visible place is important to me when shopping.	0	1	2	3	4	5
30.	Information about the present stock (special) offer of products broadcast in the media is important to me when shopping.	0	1	2	3	4	5

Short paragraph about prof. Ing. Dr. Róbert Štefko, Ph.D.

Within the area of Business Economics and Management, the author focuses on the research of marketing of intangible products, economics, and marketing management of organizations providing services and on related areas of the field. He has published important research works in the field of art marketing, marketing of selected specific areas of tourism, personnel marketing, the field of managing challenging situations in managers, especially in the context of managing marketing workers and sales representatives, sales management, and personal selling as part of marketing communication policy. Among other things, he is the originator of the marketing concept of universities in the Slovak Republic based on the so-called reproduction cycles of the quality of inputs, a system of maximizing the attractiveness of the organization in the perception of target audiences, with evaluation based on responsive models, price sensitivity testing and other concepts in this area. He is a pioneer in the implementation of related strategies in the Slovak educational competitive environment. Since his concepts were put into practice in 2004, there has been a tremendously high interest in studying at the Faculty of Management and Business, which has, in some years, had the highest interest of applicants for studies regarding the capacities in the Slovak Republic, according to the Ministry's assessment. He is a member of different organizations, i.e., DEAN, the Deans' European and Academics Network, Brussels, Belgium; NECSTouR, the Network of European Regions Committed to the Issue of Sustainable Tourism); TIIKM, the International Institute of Knowledge Management, Sri Lanka (member of the advisory board); and CMS, the Czech Marketing Society, Prague. Also, he was a member of the Scientific Board of Publication Interdisciplinary Approach to Sustainable Development edited by ISI Pierrard, HEC du Luxemburg, Virton, Belgique 2007, Belgium Depot Légal: D/2007/9727/4. Until 2006 he was a member of two working groups of the Accreditation Commission of the Slovak Accreditation Agency for Higher Education, an advisory body of the Slovak government in the field of economics and management. Nowadays, he is a member of the commission of the Scientific Grant Agency of the Ministry of Education, Science, Research and Sport of the Slovak Republic – VEGA for Economic and law sciences (no. 13). He received a Management Certificate from Wichita State University, W. Frank Barton School of Business, the USA, 27/04/1995.

Short paragraph about doc. PaedDr. Zuzana Birknerová, PhD., MBA

The rich publishing activity of the author is primarily focused on social phenomena such as social and emotional intelligence and related constructs of them, with which she usually deals in the context of managerial work. She has written a few monographs, of which two were nationwide and two overseas. She has published five national university textbooks focused on managers, such as Chapters of Social Psychology for Managers and Organizational Behavior from theory to application in practice. Significant is a current content article in the Economic Journal entitled Social Intelligence as an important predictor of managerial behavior. She has written various scientific foreign and national studies, scientific and professional works published in foreign anthologies, and professional works in peer-reviewed professional journals. She devoted time to significant Scopus' foreign scientific source called Measuring social intelligence-the MESI methodology. She has written valuable scripts and teaching texts. Her publishing activity also consists of registered reviews of national and foreign publications, as well as responses, of which there are hundred eighty-five national sources and fifty-four foreign sources. She works at the Faculty of Management and Business of the University of Presov in Presov as the Head of the Department of Managerial Psychology.

Short paragraph about PhDr. Anna Tomková, PhD.

The author also works at the Faculty of Management and Business of the University of Presov in Presov as a scientific and pedagogical worker. Within the pedagogical activity, she teaches subjects of Social Psychology, Organizational Behavior, and Business Psychology. Her research activity focuses on practice related to social behavior and psychology in business. She has collaborated on several successful scientific research projects and grants as a co-researcher.

Short paragraph about Ing. Ivana Ondrijová, PhD.

The author graduated in engineering at The Faculty of Economics of the Technical University in Slovakia in the city of Kosice. In 2016, she completed her internal doctoral studies in the field of Management at the Faculty of Management and Business of the University of Presov in Presov. Nowadays, the author works as an assistant professor at the Department of Managerial Psychology at the Faculty of Management and Business, and at the same time as the secretary of the department. Within pedagogical activities, she teaches subjects of Methodology and Business Psychology. As part of scientific and research activities, she deals with the issue of business psychology. As a co-investigator, she has collaborated on several successful scientific research projects and grants.

Short paragraph about Mgr. Dávid Miško, PhD.

The author works as a scientific worker at the Faculty of Management and Business of the University of Presov in Presov. Within pedagogical activities, he teaches subjects as Coaching and Organizational Behavior. The present research activity focuses on Neuromarketing, Coaching, Cognitive Distortions and Organizational Behavior. The author has collaborated on several successful scientific research projects and grants as a co-researcher.

Short paragraph about Mgr. Barbara Nicole Čigarská

She successfully completed bachelor's and master's studies at the Faculty of Management and Business of the University of Presov in Presov in the Management study program with a focus on business psychology, marketing and business. The author has been awarded by the Rector's Award of the University of Presov in Presov twice for well-processed final theses. The author works as an internal doctoral student at the Department of Managerial psychology at the Faculty of Management and Business of the University of Presov in Presov. Her research activity is focused on a very up-to-date topic of emotional intelligence and burnout syndrome in connection with chronic fatigue and mental resilience in the work process. Within pedagogical activities, she teaches the subject of Organizational Behavior. While studying at the Faculty of Management and Business, she participated in a study abroad within the Erasmus+ program in Latvia in the city of Valmiera at the Faculty of Society and Sciences of the Vidzeme University of Applied Sciences, and also at the Faculty of Business Administration of the Prague University of Economics and Business. At the University of Presov in Presov she humbly and honorably participates as the secretary of the Academic Senate and at the Faculty of Management and Business as a member of the Academic Senate, Council for Quality and Disciplinary commission. Also, she participates as a member of working groups of the Slovak Accreditation Agency for Higher Education.

Neuromarketing attributes in the context of determinants of business behavior and neurolinguistic programming

Authors:
prof. Ing. Dr. Róbert Štefko, Ph.D.[1,2]
doc. PaedDr. Zuzana Birknerová, PhD., MBA[1]
PhDr. Anna Tomková, PhD.[1]
Ing. Ivana Ondrijová, PhD.[1]
Mgr. Dávid Miško, PhD.[1]
Mgr. Barbara Nicole Čigarská[1]

Publisher:	© 2023 Peter Lang Group AG, Lausanne
Edition:	first
Year of publication:	2023
Print run:	110 copies
Extent:	170 pages
Press:	Peter Lang GmbH, Berlin, Deutschland

ISBN 978-3-631-89786-7

1. Faculty of Management and Business, University of Presov, Slovakia
2. PAN-EUROPEAN University in the Czech Republic (PEUNI)

www.ingramcontent.com/pod-product-compliance
Ingram Content Group UK Ltd.
Pitfield, Milton Keynes, MK11 3LW, UK
UKHW021904240426
12048UKWH00045B/646